H.P. BLAVATSKY AND THE MASTERS OF THE WISDOM

H.P. BLAVATSKY AND THE MASTERS OF THE WISDOM

BY
ANNIE BESANT

GYAN

ISBN: 978-81-212-1900-6 (HB)
First Published, 1907
Published, 2018
Published by

Gyan Publishing House
5, Ansari Road
Daryaganj, New Delhi-110002
Phone: 011-47034999, 9811692060
www.gyanbooks.com
E-mail: books@gyanbooks.com

Printed at: G. Print Process, Delhi.

H. P. BLAVATSKY.

Sixteen years and a half have gone since Helena Petrovna Blavatsky passed away from this mortal world. Yet attacks are still made upon her veracity, upon her character, and good and sympathetic men still turn away from the Theosophical Society with: "Oh! I do not care to belong to it; it was founded by Mme. Blavatsky, who was convicted of fraud by the Psychical Research Society." The articles which defended her at the time have long been out of print, and are forgotten; Dr. Hodgson, the writer of the S.P.R. report, became a believer in phenomena far more wonderful than those which he denied in his youthful self-confidence, and also became himself the victim of misrepresentation and ridicule. The large circulation of Mme. Blavatsky's priceless works, the spread of the ideas which she spent her life in learning and teaching, the growth of the Theosophical Society which she founded at the orders of her Master, and with the aid of her colleague, Colonel H. S. Olcott, the ever-increasing literature published by her pupils—all these form her substantial defence, the justification of her life's work. But it is not right that the continued crucifixion of the Teacher should be regarded with complacency, while the world profits by the teachings, nor that she should be branded as fraud and impostor who brought to this age the truths now gaining such world-wide acceptance. It is but just that her defence should be obtainable so long as she is slandered. Therefore I—who reverence her as my first Teacher, and who keep her in my heart with unceasing gratitude as the one who led me to my Master, whom I have now served with ever-increasing thankfulness for more than eighteen years—place here on record the facts of the past, with such comment as seems necessary.

Helena Petrovna was the daughter of Colonel Peter Hahn, and the grand-daughter of Lieut.-General Alexis Hahn von Rottenstein-Hahn; her mother was Helena

Fadéeff, daughter of Privy-Councillor André Fadéeff and the Princess Helena Dolgorouki. The following letter—translated from the French original, which lies before me—by Lieut.-Major-General R. Fadéeff, to A. P. Sinnett, Esq., c/o H. H. the Viceroy's Private Secretary, through the Prince Dondoukoff-Horsanoff, Governor-General of the Caucasus, testifies to her identity: "I certify by these presents that Madam Helena Petrovna Blavacki,[1] now dwelling in Simla (British India), is, on her father's side, daughter of Colonel Peter, and grand-daughter of Lieut.-General Alexis Hahn de Rottenstein-Hahn (a noble family of Mecklenburg, settled in Russia), and, on her mother's side, daughter of Helena Fadéeff, and grand-daughter of Privy-Councillor André Fadéeff, and the Princess Helena Dolgouki,[2] and that she is the widow of the Councillor of State, Nicéphore Blavacki, late Vice-Governor of the Province of Erivan (Caucasus).

Major-General ROSTISLAW FADÉEFF,
Joint Secretary of the Minister of the Interior, Count Ignatieff, Attaché of the État-Major of the Minister of War.

S. Petersbourg, Little Morskaia, 23.
18/30 September, 1881."

With this was a letter, saying that a formal Government certificate would follow in a few days.

Helena Petrovna was born in 1831, and her aunt, Madame N. A. Fadéeff, writing in Odessa on 8/20 of May, 1877, bears witness to the marvels surrounding her from childhood. Madame Fadéeff states that she had herself always been profoundly interested in psychological phenomena, and had taken every opportunity of observing them. She proceeds: "The phenomena produced by the mediumistic power of my niece Helena are very curious and wonderful, veritable marvels; but they are not exceptional or unique. Many times have I been told of, and I have often read in works dealing with spiritualism, sacred and profane, astonishing accounts of phenomena resembling those which you mention in your letter, but they have generally been isolated occurrences, or coming from different sources. But so much force concentrated in a single individual—a whole group of the most extraordinary manifestations emanating from a single source, as in the case of Madame Blavatsky—that is certainly exceedingly rare and perhaps unparallelled. I have long known her to be possessed of mediumistic power, the greatest with which

---

[1] *Anglice*, Blavatsky. [2] *Anglice*, Dolgorouki.

I have met; but when she was here this power was in a condition far inferior to that which it has now reached. My niece Helena is a being quite apart, and cannot be compared with anyone else. As child, as young girl, as woman, she was always too superior to her environment to be appreciated at her real value. She received the education of a girl of good family. She was well brought up, but was not at all learned, and as for scholarship, of that there was no question. But the unusual richness of her intellectual nature, the delicacy and swiftness of her thought, her marvellous facility in understanding, grasping and assimilating the most difficult subjects, such as would require from anybody else years of laborious study; an eminently developed intelligence, united with a character loyal, straightforward, frank, energetic—these gave her such an unusual superiority, raised her so high above the ordinary level of the insipid majority of human societies, that she could never avoid attracting general attention, and the consequent envy and animosity of all those who, in their trivial inferiority, felt wounded by the splendor of the faculties and talents of this really marvellous woman.

You ask what languages she has studied. From childhood, in addition to Russian, her native tongue, she knew only French and English. Long afterwards, during her travels in Europe, she picked up a little Italian. The last time that I saw her, four years from that time, that was all she knew in the way of languages; of that I am positively certain, I can assure you. As to the unfathomable depths of her erudition, at the time I speak of, four years after, as I say, there was no shadow of it, not even the least promise thereof. She was well brought up, well educated as a woman of the world, that is to say, very superficially. But as to serious and abstract studies, the religious mysteries of antiquity, Alexandrian Theurgy, ancient philosophies and philologies, the science of hieroglyphs, Hebrew, Samskṛiṭ, Greek, Latin, etc., she never saw them even in a dream. I can swear to it. She had not the least idea of the very alphabet of such things."

To return: Helena Petrovna was married, as a girl of seventeen, to an old man, and promptly took flight from her husband, on discovering what marriage meant, and roamed about the world in search of knowledge. In August, 1851, we find her in London, and there, on a moonlight night, as her diary tells us, beside the Serpentine, "I met the Master of my dreams." He then told her that he had chosen her to work in a society, and some time afterwards, with her father's permission, she went into training for her future mission, passing through seven and ten years of probation, trial and hard work. Mme. Fadéeff may again help us. She writes from Paris, under date June 26th, 1884: "I wrote to Mr. Sinnett two or three years ago, in answer to one of his letters, and I think that I told him what occurred in connection with a letter received by me phenomenally, when my niece was on the other side of the world, or when, to speak the fact, no one knew where she was—which was exactly the thing that troubled us. All our enquiries had ended in nothing. We were ready to believe her dead, when —I think in the year 1870, or soon after—I received a letter from the Being whom you call, I think, Kooṭ-Hoomi, which was brought to me in the most incomprehensible and mysterious way, in my own house, by a messenger with an Asiatic face, who vanished before my eyes. This letter, which begged me not to be anxious and assured me that she was safe, is still in my possession, but at Odessa. When I return I will forward it to you, and I shall be very glad if it is of use to you. Excuse me, but is difficult, almost impossible, for me to believe that there can be people sufficiently stupid to think that either my niece, or yourself, invented the men whom you call Mahâṭmâs.

"I do not know if you have long known them personally, but my niece spoke to me about them, and that very fully, years ago. She wrote to me that she had seen and reknitted her connection with several of them before she wrote her *Isis*. Why should she have invented these personages? With what object? and what good could they do her if they did not exist? Your enemies are neither wicked nor dishonest, I think; they are, if they accuse you of that, only idiotic. If I, who am, I hope, to remain to my death a fervent Christian, believe in the existence of these men—though not in all the miracles alleged about them—why should not others believe? I can certify to the existence of one of them, at least. Who could have written to reassure me in the moment when I most needed such reassurance, if it were not one of these Adepts they talk of? It is true that I do not know the writing, but the way in which it was delivered to me was so phenomenal that no one, save an adept in occult science, could have accomplished it. It promised me the return of my niece, and the promise was fulfilled. Anyhow, I will send it to you in a fortnight, and you will receive it in London."

The letter was duly forwarded ten days later, enclosed in a note from Madame Fadéeff; it was written on Chinese rice-paper, "backed with the glassy hand-made paper one sees in Kashmîr and the Panjâb, and enclosed in an envelope of the same paper. The address is: 'To the Honourable, Very Honourable, Lady Nadejka Andriewna Fadéeff, Odessa.' In one corner, in the handwriting of Madame Fadéeff, is the note in the Russian language in pencil, 'Received at Odessa, November 7th, about Lelinka (H.P.B.'s pet name), probably from Tibet. November 11th, 1870, Nadejka F.' The note says: 'The noble relatives of Madame H. Blavatsky have no cause to mourn. Their daughter and niece has not departed from this world. She lives, and wishes to make known to those she loves, that she is well, and feels very happy in the distant and unknown retreat that she has chosen. . . . Let the ladies of her family comfort themselves. Before 18 new moons have risen, she will have returned to her home.' Both the note and the envelope are written in the now familiar handwriting of the Mahâṭmâ K.H." [1]

The following dates are taken from a scrap of paper, found at Adyar, in a writing I do not recognise, and unsigned. I give them for what they are worth.

In 1848, immediately after her marriage, she left the Caucasus and went to Egypt, travelling with the Countess Kiselef. She visited Athens, Smyrna and Asia Minor, and made her first effort to enter Tibet, but failed. In 1853, at the time of the visit of the Nepaulese Embassy to London (but in 1851, according to her own diary), she was in London, and met there her Master. Thence she went to South America, and through the Pacific islands to India, and made her second ineffectual attempt to enter Tibet. She returned to England, *viâ* China, Japan and America, about 1853. She then travelled to the United States and Central America, and back to England in 1855 or '56. Thence she again went to India, *viâ* Egypt, and just before the outbreak of the Sepoys she made her third unsuccessful attempt to enter Tibet. She then disappears, turning up in Russia at the end of 1858 or beginning of 1859. She was in Tiflis from 1861 to 1863, and then went to Egypt, and thence to Persia, crossing over Central Asia and penetrated to Tibet about 1864. She paid a flying visit to Italy in 1866, and then back to India and the north, to the Kumlun mountains and Lake Palti and Tibet. She returned to Odessa, *viâ* Egypt and Greece, in 1872.

In 1872, according to the *Theosophist*, Madame Blavatsky was shipwrecked, and was given help and shelter, while awaiting remittances from Russia, by some people who were to work her much harm in later days—the Coulombs, then keeping a hotel in Cairo, Egypt. Madame Coulomb seems to have been a medium, and to have interested Madame Blavatsky. Their acquaintance was brief, for the latter

[1] *Report of the Result of an Investigation into the charges against Madame Blavatsky.* Pp. 95, 96.

shortly went on to Russia, and thence to France and America, meeting in the latter country Colonel Olcott, with whom, on November 17th, 1875, she founded, in pursuance of the order she had received, the Theosophical Society. The story of that time may be read in the *Old Diary Leaves,*[1] by Colonel Olcott, wherein is given an account of her extraordinary powers, and of the phenomena which surrounded her. From America, the two founders came to India, and fixed their headquarters for a time in Bombay. There Madame Blavatsky received a letter from Madame Coulomb, dated June 10th, 1879, telling her of the troubles she had passed through, and begging her to lend her Rs. 200[2]. In the late spring of 1880, she and her husband came to Bombay in great poverty, and Madame Blavatsky took pity on them and helped them, afterwards establishing them in the headquarters at Adyar, M. Coulomb as librarian and man-of-all-work—for the library was in the future—and Madame Coulomb as housekeeper and caretaker.

The work of Madame Blavatsky and Colonel Olcott in India is well known; the same marvels surrounded her in India as in America, and, joined to her wonderful insight into the truths underlying all religions, and her intense love for India, "the motherland of my Master," drew round her crowds of the cultured classes of India. Here, again, the *Old Diary Leaves* may be read by those who desire to see the evidence for the extraordinary strength and range of her occult powers. Her brilliant articles in the *Theosophist* show her knowledge, and the frequent appearances of the Masters and Their constant communications with her, and with those around her, became widely known. Mr. Sinnett in his *Occult World*, has placed on record his own experiences and those of the circle round him; perhaps the greatest phenomenon of all was the change effected in this sceptical Anglo-Indian, the Editor of the *Pioneer*, who, by his contact with the Master K.H., into which he was brought by Madame Blavatsky, became His faithful and loyal disciple, steadfastly serving him through all vicissitudes. [3]

If human evidence can ever substantiate a fact, the fact of the appearance of the Masters, and of the communications received from Them during these years, is placed beyond the possibility of doubt. Let me take a few at random. Mr. S.

---

[1] It would be useless to fill these pages with quotations from books now in circulation, and which can be consulted by anyone wishing to know the facts.

[2] *Report of the Result*, etc. Pp. 131, 132.

[3] As already said, I am not giving here evidence open to all in books now in circulation; any serious student can study *The Occult World*, with its invaluable information, for himself.

Râmasvâmier, a District Registrar, on December 1st., 1881, gave a note in a closed envelope to Madame Blavatsky, and then went out for a drive with her, Colonel Olcott and Damoḍar; on returning to the house they all saw, leaning over the balcony, a man, recognised by the Colonel and Damoḍar as Madame Blavatsky's Master; He raised His hand and dropped a letter to the ground; it was written in Tibetan characters, and was an answer to the note of Mr. Râmasvâmier, who certifies, under date December 28th, 1881, that Madame Blavatsky was not out of his sight from the moment he gave her his note to the time he saw the figure drop the answer. [1] Mr. and Mrs. Scott—Mr. Scott was a civil servant in India who rose to the position of Judicial Commissioner of Ouḍh—Colonel Olcott, Madame Blavatsky, Mr. M. Muraḍ Ali Beg, Mr. Damoḍar K. Mavalankar, and Paṇḍiṭ Bhavâni Shankar, were sitting together on a balcony, from which the library in partial darkness, and a room beyond brilliantly lighted, were visible. Mr. Scott saw a man, whom he recognised from His portrait, as Master M., step into the lighted room; all saw Him clearly; He walked towards a table, and on that, subsequently, a letter was found in the familiar writing. [2] Colonel Olcott writes, under date 30th September, 1881; "This same Brother once visited me in the flesh at Bombay, coming in full daylight and on horseback. He had me called by a servant into the front room of H. P. B.'s bangalow (she being at the time in the other bangalow, talking with those who were there). He came to scold me roundly for something I had done in T. S. matters, and as H. P. B. was also to blame, He telegraphed to her to come, that is to say He turned His face and extended His finger in the direction of the place she was in. She came over at once with a rush, and seeing Him dropped on her knees and paid Him reverence. My voice and His had been heard by those in the other bangalow, but only H. P. B. and I, and the servant *saw* Him. Another time two, if not three persons, sitting in the verandah of my bangalow in the Girgaum compound, saw a Hindu gentleman ride in, dismount under H. P. B.'s portico and enter her study. They called me, and I went and watched the horse until the visitor came out, remounted and rode off. That also was a Brother in flesh and bones." [3]

During this time M. and Mme. Coulomb were living in the Bombay Headquarters, and Mme. Coulomb, as a Spiritualist, was not sceptical as to the reality of the phenomena, but,

[1] *Hints on Esoteric Philosophy.* Pp. 72, 73.
[2] *Ibid.* Pp. 74-76.
[3] *Ibid.* P. 80.

as a fanatical and superstitious Christian, she considered them—they being so connected with non-Christians—as the work of the devil. Mr. Marṭanḍrao B. Nâgnâṭh, who was much with the founders at Bombay from 1879 to 1889, records instances of his seeing the "generally unseen Brothers of the 1st Section of the Theosophical Society." (The Theosophical Society, in its early days, was organised in three sections, the first section consisting of the Masters.) In 1881, he, with three brother Theosophists, was talking with Mme. Blavatsky, Mme. Coulomb being also present, when they saw the Master K. H. "about eight or ten yards distant." "He was wearing a white loose gown or robe, with long wavy hair and a beard; and was gradually forming, as it were, in front of a shrub or number of shrubs, some twenty or thirty yards away from us, until He stood to a full height. Mme. Coulomb was asked in our presence by Mme. Blavatsky: 'Is this good Brother a devil?' as she used to think and say so, when seeing the Brothers, and was afraid. She then answered: 'No, this one is a man.' He then showed His full figure for about two or three minutes, then gradually disappearing, melting away into the shrub." This statement, which contains an account of various other phenomena, is dated Bombay, 14th February, 1882.[1] It is confirmed by Paṇḍiṭ Bhavâni Shankar.[2]

After the Headquarters of the Society were moved to Aḍyar, Maḍras (Dec. 30th, 1882), similar appearances of the Masters frequently took place: it was a household custom for the workers to gather on the flat roof in the evening, and thither, now and again, would come a Master visibly, and graciously talk with and instruct them. On this, Mr. C. W. Leadbeater, who was working at Aḍyar and elsewhere in India and Ceylon for the Society from 1884 to 1888, writes as follows: "I am very glad to testify that I have on many occasions seen the Masters appear in materialised form at the Headquarters at Aḍyar. Under such conditions I have seen the Master M., the Master K. H., the Master D. K., and also another member of the Brotherhood, besides one or two pupils who acted as messengers. Such appearances occurred sometimes on the flat roof of the main building, sometimes in my own room by the riverside, and on several occasions in the garden. The materialisations were frequently maintained for twenty minutes, and on at least two occasions for considerably over half-an-hour."

These appearances of the Masters were not, however, confined to the Headquarters at Bombay and at Madras.

---

[1] *Hints on Esoteric Philosophy*. P. 105. [2] *Report of the Result*, etc. Pp. 76, 77.

Mr. T. Brown states the following in *My Experiences in India.* "Lahore has a special interest, because there we saw, in his own physical body, Mahâṭmâ Kooṭ Hoomi himself. On the afternoon of the 19th November, I saw the Master in broad daylight, and recognised him, and on the morning of the 20th he came to my tent and said: 'Now you see me before you in the flesh: look, and assure yourself that it is I,' and left a letter of instructions and a silk handkerchief, both of which are now in my possession. The letter is as usual written seemingly with blue pencil, is in the same handwriting as that in which is written the communication received at Maḍras, and has been identified by about a dozen persons as bearing the caligraphy of Mahâṭmâ Kooṭ Hoomi. The letter was to the effect that I had first seen him in visions, then in his astral form, then in body at a distance, and that finally I now saw him in his own physical body, so close to me as to enable me to give to my countrymen the assurance that I was, from personal knowledge, as sure of the existence of the Mahâṭmâs as I was of my own. The letter is a private one, and I am not enabled to quote from it at length. On the evening of the 21st, Colonel Olcott, Damoḍar and I were sitting outside the shamiâna, when we were visited by . . . . (the Master's head Chelâ, now an Initiate), who informed us that the Master was about to come. The Master then came near to us, gave instructions to Damoḍar, and walked away."[1]

Of this same visit to Lahore, November, 1883, Damoḍar himself gives many details. Of the Mahâṭmâ K.H. he says: "There I was visited by Him in body, for three nights consecutively, for about three hours every time, while I myself retained full consciousness, and in one case even went to meet Him outside the house. Him whom I saw in person at Lahore was the same I had seen in astral form at the Ḥeadquarters of the Theosophical Society, and the same again whom I, in visions and trances, had seen at His house, thousands of miles off, to reach which in my astral Ego I was permitted, owing, of course, to His direct help and protection. In those instances, with my psychic powers hardly developed yet, I had always seen Him as a rather hazy form, although His features were perfectly distinct, and their remembrance was profoundly graven on my soul's eye and memory. While now at Lahore, Jammu, and elsewhere, the impression was utterly different. In the former cases, when making pranâm (salutation) my hands passed through His form, while on the latter occasions they met solid garments and flesh. Here I

[1] *Report of the Result*, etc. Pp. 74, 75.

saw *a living man* before me, the same in features, though far more imposing in His general appearance and bearing than Him I had so often looked upon in the portrait in Mme. Blavatsky's possession, and in the one with Mr. Sinnett. I shall not here dwell upon the fact of His having been corporeally seen by both Colonel Olcott and Mr. Brown separately, for two nights at Lahore, as they can do so better, each for himself, if they so choose. At Jammu again, where we proceeded from Lahore, Mr. Brown saw Him on the evening of the third day of our arrival there, and from Him received a letter in His familiar handwriting, not to speak of His visits to me almost every day, and what happened the next morning almost everyone in Jammu is aware of. The fact is, that I had the good fortune of being sent for, and permitted to visit a sacred Âshrama, where I remained for a few days in the blessed company of several of the Mahâṭmâs of Himavaṭ and Their disciples. There I met not only my beloved Guruḍeva and Colonel Olcott's Master, but several others of the Fraternity, including one of the highest. I regret the extremely personal nature of my visit to those regions prevents my saying more of it. Suffice it that the place I was permitted to visit is in the Himâlayas, not in any fanciful summer land, and that I saw Him in my own sthûlasharira (physical body), and found my Master identical with the form I had seen in the earlier days of my Chelâship. Thus I saw my beloved Guru not only as a *living* man, but actually as a young one in comparison with some other Sâḍhus of the blessed company, only far kinder, and not above a merry remark and conversation at times. Thus, on the second day of my arrival, after the meal hour, I was permitted to hold an intercourse for over an hour with my Master. Asked by Him smilingly what it was that made me look at Him so perplexed, I asked in my turn: "How is it, Master, that some of the members of our Society have taken into their heads a notion that you were 'an elderly man,' and that they have even seen you clairvoyantly, looking an old man past sixty?" To which He pleasantly smiled and said that this latest misconception was due to the reports of a certain Brahmachâri, a pupil of a Vedânṭic Svâmi in the N.W.P., who had met last year in Tibet the chief of a sect, an elderly Lâma, who was His (my Master's) travelling companion at that time. The said Brahmachâri, having spoken of the encounter in India, had led several persons to mistake the Lâma for Himself. As to His being perceived clairvoyantly as 'an elderly man,' that could never be, He added, as *real* clairvoyance could lead no one into such a mistaken notion, and then He kindly reprimanded me for giving any importance to the age of a Guru, adding that appearances were often false, etc., and explaining other points." [1]

Paṇḍiṭ Bhavâni Shankar says that while travelling in the North in the spring of 1884, Mahâṭmâ M. was seen by Mr. Nivaraṇ Chandra Mukerji and himself, in His astral body, at a Branch meeting, and goes on: "I have seen the same Mahâṭmâ, *viz.*, Madame Blavatsky's Master, several times in His double during my travels in the North. Not only have I seen Madame Blavatsky's Master in His double, but also my venerated Gurudeva K.H. I have also seen the latter, *viz.*, my Master, in His physical body, and recognised Him." [2]

Mr. Mohini M. Chatterji. writing on September 30th, 1884, says: "To a Brâhmaṇa, like myself, it is repugnant to speak of the sacredly confidential relationship existing between a spiritual teacher and his pupil. Yet, duty compels me in this instance to say that I have personal and absolute knowledge of the existence of the Mahâṭmâ, who has corresponded with Mr. Sinnett, and is known to the Western world as 'Koot Hoomi.' I had knowledge of the Mahâṭmâ in question before I knew Mme. Blavatsky, and I met Him in person when He passed through the Madras Presidency to China—last year." [3]

Mr. S. Râmasvâmier, setting off to Tibet in search of his Guru, was met on the road to Sikkim by "a solitary horseman, galloping towards me from the opposite direction. . . . As He approached me, He reined in His steed. I looked at Him, and recognised Him instantly. I was in the presence of the same Mahâṭmâ, my own revered Guru, whom I had seen before in His astral body, on the balcony of the Theosophical Headquarters. It was He of the ever-memorable night of December 1st, who had dropped a letter in answer to one I had given in a sealed envelope to Madame Blavatsky—whom I had never for one moment during the interval lost sight of—but an hour or so before. . . . I was at last face to face with the 'Mahâṭmâ of the Himavaṭ,' and He was no myth, no 'creation of the imagination.' It was not night; it was between nine and ten o'clock of the forenoon. My happiness made me dumb." [4] Mr. R. Casava Pillai also, near Sikkim, "saw the Mahâṭmâs in their physical bodies, and found them to be identical with those whom he had seen in dreams and visions, or in astral form as above stated" (in Bombay). [5]

---

[1] *Report of the Result*, etc. Pp. 82-84.

[2] *Report of the Result*, etc. Pp. 79, 80. [3] *Ibid.* P. 74.

[4] *Report of the Result*, etc. Pp. 85, 86.

[5] *Ibid.* P. 89.

Here we have a number of independent witnesses, bearing testimony to their meeting these same Masters in the flesh.

Leaving now the direct manifestations of the Masters, I select from among the numerous communications received in a superphysical manner from Them, the following, merely as illustrations: at Bombay, on the 2nd February, 1882, the Hon. J. Smith, member of the Legislative Council, N.S.W., Professor in Sydney University, went with Madame Blavatsky into his own bedroom, he having first entered it alone and seen that it was as usual; they sat down together, and in doing so "she took my hands in both of hers. In a few seconds a letter fell at my feet. It seemed to me to appear first a little above the level of my head. On opening the envelope I found a sheet of note-paper headed with a Government stamp of the North-Western Provinces and Oudh, and the following words written with red pencil, in exactly the same hand-writing as that in the letters of the previous evening: 'No chance of writing to you inside your letters, but I can write *direct*. Work for us in Australia, and we will not prove ungrateful, but will prove to you our actual existence, and thank you.' A fair review of the circumstances excludes, in my opinion, any theory of fraud. J. SMITH." Prof. Smith, later, writing from Nice to Madame Blavatsky, under date of January 31st, 1883, gives the following account of a communication received by him: "You think that my note to M. was a failure, but let me now tell you the facts. You may remember that you concluded your letter with a P. S. requesting me not to be angry with the Brother. This was followed by a few words in red ink in M.'s hand, to the effect that your advice was very kind and considerate (evidently sarcastic). But more than that. Inside your letter was a small envelope, curiously folded and gummed and addressed to me in red. On cutting this open, I found my own little note to M. *absolutely intact*. My wife, who sewed it up, and other ladies to whom I shewed it, are satisfied that the stitching had never been disturbed. At first I was inclined to think that it had come back just as it went, but on cutting it open, what was the astonishment of all of us when I drew out a piece of Chinese paper with a curious picture on it, and some writing in red ink round the margin, with M.'s signature or rather cryptograph. The sentence began: 'Your ladies, I see, are unbelievers, and they are better needlewomen than our Hindu and Tibetan lasses,' etc. To me and my wife the test is as satisfactory as it is gratifying and astonishing. How did that Chinese paper get inside my note? Not by any means known to ordinary mortals. I scarcely dared to hope for anything so good when

I enclosed the note to M., and I am very grateful to him for it. I am encouraged to enclose another note for him in the hope of getting a reply, but I do not make it any test. I wish only for information. But if he should see fit, voluntarily, to give me some additional proof of his 'miraculous' powers (for with our received notions of matter this affair of the note may be so designated) I shall be intensely pleased. I am more than ever sorry that I did not stay with you a week longer, that I might have had a chance of seeing M., and perhaps becoming personally acquainted with him. When you mention the disappearance of my note to M., you add: 'To all my questions I received one reply: "Mind your business," etc.' In what way were the questions made? By mental impressions simply? Or in actual conversations with M.'s double or projection? And do you know why M. took away my letter to you as well as the note to himself? (that is, supposing he *did* take it), for by so doing your answer to me and his own communication to me, were greatly delayed. . . . My wife desires me to send you her very kind regards. She hopes to see you sometime. You say you trust she will then *believe* a little more than she does. But I think I told you that she believed the facts included under the term Spiritualism, and now she is quite satisfied with this test sent by M., feeling sure that by no known means could that piece of Chinese paper have been inserted into the note sewn up by her."

I have in my hands many of the letters sent by the Masters during these years, some scribbled down on the letter requiring the answer, some independent. They came in all ways—by post, by sudden appearance on a table, in a drawer, falling through the air, etc. On February 10th, 1882, a letter was seen to fall to the ground perpendicularly, in the open air, ten paces from Mme. Blavatsky's chair, and seven from the little group who saw it fall. Another fell in a railway carriage, containing Mme. Blavatsky, Mr. and Mrs. Oakley and Mr. Leadbeater, blaming her for what she was doing at the moment. But the instances are innumerable. The phenomenal delivery of letters was by no means confined to Mme. Blavatsky's immediate neighborhood. Dr. Hartmann tells us that a pair of pincers was wanted, and "remembering that I had such a pair of pincers in the drawer of my writing desk, I went down stairs into my room to get them. I opened the drawer, saw the pincers and a few other things in there, but no vestige of any letter, as I had removed my papers the day before to another place. I took the pincers and was about to close the drawer, when—there lay *in the drawer* a great envelope, addressed to me in the well-known handwriting of the Master and sealed with the seal bearing His initials in Tibetan characters. On opening it, I found a long, very kind letter treating of the identical questions, about which I had just been talking with Mme. Blavatsky,[1] besides giving a detailed and very satisfactory answer to the very question which had so perplexed my mind, and a satisfactory explanation of certain matters, which for some time had been foremost in my mind, but of which I had said nothing at all. Moreover there was in the same envelope a photograph, cabinet-size, of the Master's face, with a dedication to me at the back. Now, if I know anything at all, I know that my drawer contained no such letter when I opened it, and that there was nobody visible in my room at that time. The letter, giving a detailed answer to my question, must have been written, sealed and put into the drawer in less than four minutes, while it took exactly forty minutes to copy it the next day; and finally, it treated a very difficult problem in such an elaborate and yet concise manner, that only an intelligence of the highest order could have done the same (February 5th, 1884)."[2]

On the 17th March, 1884, Mr. Navaṭram Ooṭaram Trivedi, was at the Headquarters, Aḍyar, and wrote out some questions on a sheet of foolscap: "I wanted Damoḍar to have the questions answered, but he did not take any notice of them. At about noon I sat at a table, with Mr. Damodar opposite to me. This was in the office room downstairs. I read over to myself the questions that I had written out, and laid the paper upon the table. In a few minutes, while I was talking to Damoḍar, the paper disappeared, and I silently remarked this, but I kept on talking, and in a short while an envelope was found lying upon the floor. It was addressed to me, and, on opening it, I found my own sheet of questions written over in blue pencil. The answers to my questions were full, and had been written close to each of the questions on my own paper. The handwriting was that of Mahâṭmâ K. H. Madame Blavatsky and Colonel Olcott were then not at Aḍyar, but had proceeded to Europe, and were probably in Paris."[3]

Says Mr. R. Casava Pillai: "In the year 1882, while I was travelling by railway between the Allahabâḍ and Mogal

[1] He had broken off his conversation with Madame Blavatsky in order to go downstairs for the pincers.

[2] *Report of Observations made during a nine months' stay at the Headquarters of the T.S.* By F. Hartmann, M.D. Pp. 29-30.

[3] *Report of the Result*, etc. Pp. 61, 62. The questions and answers are printed in the *Theosophist* for July, 1907. I copied them from the original document.

Serai stations, a letter fell in the compartment of the railway carriage in which I was sitting. I was alone in the compartment, and the carriage was in motion. I had wished that Mahâṭmâ K. H. should give me instructions regarding a certain matter about which I was then thinking, and when I opened the letter I found that my thoughts had been answered, and that the letter was in the handwriting of Mahâṭmâ K. H., whose writing I know so well. Madame Blavatsky was then in Bombay."[1]

As Madame Blavatsky once wrote on the margin of such an account: "Who was the fraud here?"

When Paṇḍiṭ Bhavâni Shankar was staying at Mr. Sinnett's house in Allahabâḍ, in March, 1882, Madame Blavatsky was in Bombay. Mr. Sinnett one evening gave him a note addressed to the Mahâṭmâ K. H. The Paṇḍiṭ put the letter near his pillow, locked his doors, lighted his lamp, and was alone. Between ten and eleven he saw his Master astrally, and He took the letter. The next morning he found the answer under his pillow, addressed to Mr. Sinnett, and handed it to him. On the 8th of November, 1883, at Bareilly, Paṇḍiṭ Bhavâni was talking with a European friend. He had a courier-bag hanging across his shoulder, and during the conversation he received, inside this bag, a letter from his Master, in a Chinese envelope.[2]

Damoḍar gives an account of various letters received by him, altogether apart from Madame Blavatsky. Towards the end of 1880, at Headquarters, some days after Madame Blavatsky had gone, he received from his father a letter about family business, which caused him much thought; he wrote down the decision he had come to, hoping the Mahâṭmâs would note on it whether he were right or wrong, and locked it away in his table drawer; then, thinking that if he were making a mistake, he would be corrected, he opened the drawer and destroyed his note. The next morning he found in the drawer a letter from his Master in Hinḍi. On August 21st, 1881, he was in Bombay, at Headquarters; Colonel Olcott was in Ceylon, Madame Blavatsky in Simla. One evening he was sitting near his bed, feeling very despondent because of family troubles; he saw forming, on a little table in front of him, a letter, which proved to be from his Master. In 1882, Madame Blavatsky being in Darjeeling, he was sitting in the open balcony, thinking over an idea that had come into his mind. On this occasion he was not alone; M.

---

[1] *Report of the Result*, etc. Pp. 60, 61.

[2] *Report of the Result*, etc. Pp. 77-79.

Coulomb was there. As the latter was lighting his cigarette, Damoḍar felt a slight electric shock, and saw a letter lying at his feet ; it contained a reply to his thought, as well as some information to be sent to a brother Theosophist. During Madame Blavatsky's absence in Ooṭacamunḍ, in July, 1883, various letters were received in the Shrine at Aḍyar, Damoḍar placing them within it and taking out the replies. He also received letters in the well-known writing before and after the coming of the Coulombs, away from Headquarters as well as in them, and notes written on letters from others, delivered into his own hands by the postman.[1] In all these cases, Madame Blavatsky was away, but the writing was identical with that of the letters so often received through her instrumentality.

On the 1st August, 1884, Madame Blavatsky being in England, Colonel Olcott and Dr. Hübbe-Schleiden were travelling from Elberfeld to Dresden by express. As the latter partly rose from his seat to hand the railway tickets to the guard, Colonel Olcott noticed something white lying on the seat; it turned out to be a Tibetan envelope, in which was a letter from Mahâṭmâ K.H. in His well-known writing.

Before dealing with the communications received during a short time in the famous "Shrine" at Aḍyar, it is necessary to describe the rooms which afterwards became famous. Madame Blavatsky occupied two out of the three rooms on the upper storey, opening on to a large hall. There was a sitting-room, which opened into a bedroom, and this again into a third room; the wall between the bedroom and this third room was made of two partitions with twelve inches between them, lightly built, there being no support below, and with a door in the middle, the door being thus sunk in a recess. This third room was set apart for occult purposes, and was called the Occult Room. On the partition wall, loosely hanging, was a cupboard, originally over the door,[2] in which were placed two pictures of the Masters, a silver bowl, and other articles ; the cupboard had a solid back and

---

[1] *Ibid.* Pp. 103-116.

[2] Mrs. Morgan, the wife of General Morgan, said: "I can state for a fact, that during my stay at Adyar, during December, 1883, Madame Blavatsky took Mr. C. and myself and showed us the back of the shrine, and the wall she had built behind it, where there had been a door, and the people were welcome to inspect this and see it was barred and bolted ; yet she thought it would remove the least occasion for suspicion were it bricked up, and so had it done. The wall then presented a fine, highly polished, white surface. This wall I shortly afterwards saw papered, as I superintended the hanging of the paper."—*Report of the Result*, etc Pp. 99, 100.

shelves, and was merely hung on the wall, so that it could be removed easily. This cupboard was called "The Shrine." The wall was smoothly plastered over, and various people—after it had been tampered with by the Coulombs—bore witness to the fact that at least up to February 17th, 1884—H.P.B. left Adyar on February 7th—it was intact. General Morgan states that he first saw the Occult Room in August, 1883, when he visited Adyar in Madame Blavatsky's absence, and, probably in consequence of a remarkable phenomenon that happened on his visit, he examined the Shrine and its surroundings with great care; he affirms that, up to January, 1884, when he left the Headquarters, "any trickery was impossible."

Colonel Olcott carries the date up to the 15th February, 1884, a week after Madame Blavatsky had left Adyar. On the 15th December, 1883, he had been told to try a certain experiment by making some marks "on the spots of the wall corresponding to the centre and four corners of the cupboard." He removed the shrine for this purpose, and, having made his experiment, rehung it in its place. After the Anniversary, he went to Ceylon, returning to Adyar on February 13th, 1884, *i.e.*, after Madame Blavatsky's departure, and leaving again to join her on February 15th. During this time he again took down the shrine in order to examine the marks, and at that date he found no hole in the wall. [1] It must be remembered, in this connexion, that no one has ever made the slightest imputation on Colonel Olcott's honor. He has been called a dupe, but never an accomplice.

The testimony as to the nature of the Shrine, and of the wall behind it, is overwhelming.

Judge Sir S. Subramania Aiyer, of the High Court, Madras, is perhaps the most highly respected Indian in Madras, honored alike by Europeans and Indians. He states (January 10th, 1884), that he was present at Adyar during the Anniversary of 1883, and saw certain phenomena there on the 26th and 28th of December. "The room in question is situated upstairs. In the room is the shrine—a wooden cupboard, put up against a wall. It is not fixed to the wall, but only touches it. I have carefully examined the shrine inside and outside, and also the wall against which it is put. I found nothing to suspect the existence of any contrivances which could account for what I saw. Inside the cupboard are two framed likenesses of two of the Mahâṭmâs overhung with pieces of yellow silk, a silver bowl and some images. . . .

---

[1] *Report of a Result*, etc. P. 102.

I saw no room for deception, no wire, no springs inside or outside the shrine. I requested permission to examine the shrine and was allowed to do so. Not only did I not see any wire, or spring, or any contrivance, but I *felt* none when I put my hand into the shrine, and examined it." [1]

Mr. R. Casava Pillai, an Inspector of Police, states: "When I was at the Headquarters at Aḍyar last January (1883), I went into the Occult Room five or six times. Of these, on four occasions during daytime. On two of these occasions during the day, there happened to come into the room several Theosophists from Southern India, who were desired by Madame Blavatsky on one occasion, and Mr. Damoḍar on the other, to examine the shrine and the walls of the room. These persons, after very careful examination, found nothing suspicious. The shrine was found attached to a solid wall behind, and there were no wires or other contrivances which could escape the trained eye of a police officer like myself, who was watching close by."—R. Casava Pillai. [2]

A Government Engineer writes:—" I went to the Headquarters of the Theosophical Society, at Aḍyar, on 5th July, 1883. I examined the rear, top, bottom, and side planking of the shrine, as also the walls in its vicinity, most carefully and minutely, and found no cause to suspect fraud."—C. Sambiah Chetty. [3]

The value of the evidence of the Editor of the *Philosophic Inquirer*, Mr. P. Ruṭhnavelu, is great, because he examined the shrine and its surroundings before *and after* the missionary attack. He writes: "I witnessed a phenomenon (on 1st April, 1883), a full account of which was published by me in the *Philosophic Inquirer* of the 8th April, 1883. I went up to the shrine with two sceptical friends of mine, and the doors were opened for me to inspect closely. I carefully examined everything, touching the several parts with my hand. There was no opening or hole on this side of the cupboard. I was then led into the adjoining room to see the other side of the wall to which the shrine is attached. There was a large almirah[4] standing against this wall, but it was removed at my request, that I might see the wall from that side. I tapped it and otherwise examined it, to see if there was no deception, but I was thoroughly satisfied that no deception was possible.

"On 14th September, 1884, after reading the missionary

---

[1] *Report of the Result*, etc. Pp 63, 64.

[2] *Report of the Result*, etc. P. 97. [3] *Ibid*. P. 99.

[4] *Anglice*, wardrobe.

article, I again went to see the room at 8 a.m., and was met by Mr. Judge, Dr. Hartmann and Mr. Damodar, who took me upstairs. On the other side of the wall, at the back of the shrine, I saw close to the wall an ingenious furniture-like apparatus, to which was fastened a sliding door, which, when opened, showed a small aperture in the wall. Inside of this there was hollow space, large enough for a lean lad to stand in, if he could but creep into it through the aperture, and hold his breath for a few seconds. I attempted in vain to creep in through the opening, and afterwards stretched out my hand with difficulty into the small hollow, to see the internal structure. *There was no communication* with the back-board of the Shrine. I could see that the machinery had not been finished, and the sliding panels, etc., all bore the stamp of the freshness of unfinished work."[1]

Professor J. N. Unwalla, a Parsî gentlemen of high education and standing, bears witness: "In May, 1883, when I was a guest at the Headquarters, I had many opportunities of being in the Occult Room, and of examining it and the Shrine, and once I very carefully examined the Shrine at the desire of Madame Blavatsky, before and after the occurrence of a phenomenon that I saw. I can safely say, without any equivocation or reservation, that in the Occult Room or anywhere within the precincts of the Headquarters, I never could find any apparatus or appliances of any kind suggestive of fraud or tricks."[2]

I might add to these statements, but it seems scarcely worth while to do so; they are already so conclusive. But the facts are important, as the first part of the Coulomb plot, and of Mr. Hodgson's Report, centred in and round the Shrine.

A few phenomena, out of the many connected with it, may be put on record here, though it may be remarked that the Shrine was in existence but a short time, and played no part in the great majority of the phenomena connected with Madame Blavatsky.

Of one of these, General Morgan has written an account. It occurred in August, 1883. Madame Blavatsky, then at Ooṭacamunḍ, had asked him to look at the picture in the Shrine, as it was a very peculiar work. Madame Coulomb took him upstairs, and they went into the Occult Room. "On entering the room she hurriedly approached the shrine or cupboard, and quickly opened the double doors. As she did so, a China saucer, which appeared to have been placed leaning against the door, fell down on to the chunam floor, and was

---

[1] *Ibid.* Pp. 97, 98.
[2] *Ibid.* Pp. 102, 103.

broken to pieces. On this she exhibited great consternation, exclaiming that it was a much cherished article of Madame's, and she did not know what she should do. She and her husband, who had come with us, picked up the pieces. She then tied them up in a cloth and replaced them in the shrine, *in* the silver bowl, *not behind* it. The doors were shut, and Damodar took up his position on a chair right in front of the shrine, and only a few feet distant from it. He sat intently regarding the shrine, and in a listening attitude. I was not then aware, as I am now, of the fact that the astral electric current causes a sound exactly like that of the ordinary telegraph to be distinctly heard in the shrine. Unaware of this, I resumed conversation with the Coulombs regarding the accident. When I remarked, that it would be well if he got some mastic or glue and tried to put the pieces together, he started to get some, which, he said, he had in his bangalow, situated about 100 yards from the house; and I, turning to his wife, remarked: 'If the matter is of sufficient importance, the Mahâṭmâs could cause its repair. If not, you must do the best you can.' Hardly had I uttered this, when Damodar said: 'There is a message,' and he immediately opened the door of the shrine, and took down the silver bowl (in which the letters are generally found), and sure enough there was a note, which, on opening, contained the following lines:

"'To the small audience present as witnesses. Now, Madame Coulomb has occasion to assure herself that the devil is neither as black nor as wicked as he is generally represented. The mischief is easily repaired.—K.H.'

"We then opened the cloth containing the broken saucer, found it intact and whole! *Three* minutes had not elapsed since I had suggested that the glue should be procured! and shortly after, Coulomb returned with the glue in his hand. If he could have gone all round the upper rooms, got behind the shrine, removed the broken saucer, tied up the parcel, having placed a whole one in its stead and written the note regarding the repair of the saucer (my remark about which he had not heard), then, I say, his feat rivalled that of the Masters. When I spoke to the woman about the wonderful manner in which the saucer had been restored, she replied: 'It must be the work of the devil.'" And, in fact, she wrote to Madame Blavatsky (13th Aug., 1883), that "I verily believe I shall go silly if I stay with you." She then gives an account of what had happened, and concludes: "I say you have dealings with old Nick."[1]

[1] *Reply to a Report of an Examination by J. D. B. Gribble.* By H. R. Morgan, Major-General. Pp. 14-17.

Another case was that of Judge Srînivâsa Rao, and he states as follows: "On the 4th March, 1884 (Madame Blavatsky and Colonel Olcott were at this time on the ocean, having left Bombay on Feb. 20th, for Marseilles) I, owing to certain domestic afflictions, felt exceedingly miserable all day." He went to Aḍyar, and on seeing Damoḍar, said he wished to see the Shrine. "He conducted me to the Occult Room upstairs forthwith, and unlocked the Shrine. He and I were standing hardly five seconds looking at the Mahâṭmâ K. H.'s portrait in the Shrine, when he (Mr. Damoḍar) told me that he had orders to close the Shrine, and did so immediately. This was extremely disappointing to me. But Mr. Damoḍar re-opened in an instant the Shrine. My eye immediately fell upon a letter in a Tibetan envelope in the cup in the Shrine, which was quite empty before. I took the letter, and finding that it was addressed to me by Mahâṭmâ K. H., I opened and read it." [1]

Judge Sir S. Subramania Aiyer bears witness to another phenomenon produced for the benefit of this same Mr. Srînivâsa Rao; he says: "On the 28th Dec., 1883, I went to the Shrine at 10-30 a.m. Seven persons were present. The windows were open, and it was broad daylight. Madame Blavatsky gave the key of the Shrine to Mr. P. Srinivâsa Rao, Small Cause Judge, Maḍras, and stood aside amongst us. Mr. Srînivâsa Rao opened the Shrine, took out the silver bowl, and showed it to all present. There was nothing in it. He put it into the Shrine, locked it and kept the key. About five minutes after, he was told by Madame Blavatsky to open the Shrine, which he did. He then took out the self-same silver bowl, and in it was an envelope well gummed, addressed to Mr. Srînivâsa Rao. I saw him open the envelope, and found it to contain a letter in the handwriting of Mahâṭmâ K. H., and currency notes for Rs. 500." [2]

Judge T. Râmachanḍra Rao and Mr. R. Ranga Rao went into the Occult Room: "We examined all very carefully, and the Shrine was locked. We did not, however, move from the place, and within half a minute, Madame Blavatsky told us to open it. We did so ourselves, and found the whole cupboard—where there was nothing when we looked at it half a minute before—filled with fresh flowers and leaves. Each of us took a number of them, and we found that there were also some peculiar kind of leaves which could not be found in any part of Maḍras, to our knowledge. We made a careful

---

[1] *Report of the Result*, etc. P. 59.

[2] *Ibid*. Pp. 63, 64.

survey of the whole room and its surroundings, and found nothing to warrant or justify any suspicion of trickery. T. RÂMACHANDRA RAO.

"The phenomenon, as described above, took place in my presence. R. RANGA RAO.[1]"

Madame Coulomb, in consequence of her jealous and intriguing nature, had been a source of great trouble at Headquarters, and was much disliked by the inmates. Dr. Hartmann, who arrived at Aḍyar on December 4th, 1883, gives a vivid picture of her. "Imagine a weird witchlike creature, with wrinkled features, a stinging look and an uncouth form. Her duty was to patronise the servants, to nurse like a mother a decrepit old horse and several mangy dogs which were unable to walk. She seemed to consider it her special purpose of life to pry into everybody's private affairs, pick up stray letters here and there, that were not addressed to her, probably for the purpose of studying the handwriting; she attempted to wriggle herself into the confidence of new-comers, and had a way of finding out their secrets by pretending to tell their fortunes by means of a pack of cards, while at the same time she would try to awaken the sympathies of strangers by her tales, how from a life of luxury she had sunk down to a position of servitude, and if she found a willing ear she would never hesitate a moment to insinuate that the whole Society was a humbug, the phenomena produced by fraud, and 'that she could tell many things if she only wanted to do so.' She would tell the aspirant for Theosophical honours kindly and confidentially that Colonel Olcott was a fool, who was led by the nose by Madame Blavatsky. If asked to explain herself she would say: 'My mouth is shut up, I cannot talk against the people whose bread I eat,' and when she was told that occult phenomena occurred when Madame Blavatsky was a thousand miles away, she would say that 'She knew what she knew.'[2]" It should perhaps be remembered as some sort of excuse for Madame Coulomb, that she was a superstitious Christian, and was really alarmed by the things that took place around her; she, as we have seen, believed the phenomena to be "of the devil." On the other hand, it was paradise to her to live at Aḍyar in comfort, after all her troubles, and she could not summon up courage to leave her refuge: perhaps her treachery to her benefactors was at least partly the result of a belated and distorted conscience. The temptation to remain was too

---

[1] *Ibid.* Pp. 68, 69.

[2] *Report of Observations.* P. 25.

great. Dr. Hartmann proceeds: "She had arrived at Headquarters penniless, and had been taken into the house by Madame Blavatsky, out of charity, and been given full control over everything, including the purse; and when she left the Headquarters she sported a large roll of bank-notes. (The household expenses at the Headquarters since the Coulombs left have been each month 230 to 270 rupees less than the monthly expenses during their presence)." Besides, there were many generous visitors, and "loans" could be obtained; the failure to gain one of these led to the catastrophe. Prince Harisinghji, of Kaṭhiawâr, cousin of the Mahârâja of Bhavnagar, was at the Convention of December, 1883, and Madame Coulomb approached him with a request for a loan Rs. 2000. The Prince evaded the request, saying that perhaps he would help her some day, and departed to his home.

On February 7th, 1884, Madame Blavatsky left Adyar, and as she proposed to pay a visit to Prince Harisinghji before going to Bombay *en route* for Europe, Madame Coulomb asked, and was permitted, to go with her. After arriving at the Prince's house, Madame Coulomb renewed her attack on his purse, pleading that he had promised to help her, and the Prince complained at last to Madame Blavatsky, who promptly crushed the proceedings. Dr. Hartmann, who was present, remarks: "Her fury knew no bounds, and her passionate outbursts of anger and jealousy were in no way soothed down by Madame Blavatsky reproaching her for her unjust attempt at extortion. . . . . A few tears shed by Madame Coulomb, with the assistance of a handkerchief, set the matter all right, and we proceeded to Bombay, where we met Colonel Olcott and Mr. St. George Lane-Fox, the well-known electrician, while Madame Coulomb went to visit some bishop and other clergymen, whose names are unknown to me."[1] Dr. Hartmann caustically remarks, that when Colonel Olcott and Madame Blavatsky embarked, on February 21st: "One more sob, one more embrace, and Madame Coulomb, with red eyes and faltering steps, moved out of the cabin. Stepping into her boat, she waved a last adieu to Babula, the servant of Madame Blavatsky, and said to him: 'I shall be revenged on your mistress for preventing me from getting my 2000 rupees!'"[2] The said Babula later stated: "When Madame Coulomb was leaving the steamer after bidding Madame Blavatsky good-bye, she, Madame Coulomb, said that she would be revenged on my mistress for preventing Harisinghji from giving her, Madame Coulomb, two thousand

---

[1] *Ibid.* P. 31. [2] *Ibid.* P. 32.

rupees. . . . . On another occasion, in Dr. Dudley's house in Bombay, she said that she hated Madame Blavatsky."[1] Major-General H. R. Morgan writes, as follows, about the Coulombs: "They were received by Madame Blavatsky, at Bombay, in a penniless state; were befriended by her, because they had rendered her some assistance in Egypt. The woman Coulomb became a sort of confidential housekeeper, and, as Mr. Gribble truly remarks, was the cause of Mr. Wimbridge and Miss Bates leaving the Society at Bombay. By this we see she began her malicious interference early.

"That malice is her chief characteristic I will show by the following: When at Bombay she tried to sell her knowledge of the Society to the *Guardian*, a Bombay paper, when she could have known very little, and when the correspondence now sold to the *Christian College Magazine* was not in existence nor the false phenomena which she now records; it is evident she was, so long ago as 1879, prepared with fabricated letters and phenomena. At that very time her Machiavellian nature prompted her to prepare for the downfall of her benefactor, for she asserted to more than one Theosophist that she had never thrown away a slip of Madame Blavatsky's writing, and had been the lucky finder of mischievous letters blown to her feet by the wind! Why should she have laid such store by these scraps when she was the possessor of the voluminous correspondence she has now so profitably disposed of? When we consider the characteristics of this woman, her eaves-dropping, purloining of letters, her hatred of the members composing the Society, her swearing she would be revenged, her incessant espionage of Madame Blavatsky, and those she might be talking with, the motive and manner of her concocting these letters is not difficult to understand. Her malice carried itself to such an extent that she actually kept a pack of mangy diseased dogs to worry the high caste Brahmins, and drive them away. Her object was to have sole possession of the purse, and access to the purses of others, and when her little plans were frustrated by Madame Blavatsky, she hated her accordingly.

"It may be asked why any single member of the Society tolerated her, knowing all this. The answer is—that she is a Spiritualist of the most pronounced character, is given to practising black magic, and is believed to be obsessed. Hence she was tolerated as a person hardly responsible for her actions. Added to all this, her habit of confiding her hatred of the Society and its objects, under the seal of secrecy, closed

---

[1] *Report of the Result*, etc. Pp. 133, 134.

the mouths of many who would otherwise have exposed her, and have demanded her expulsion. Further, the exceeding kind-heartedness of Colonel Olcott, and Madame Blavatsky, made them overlook many of her faults, and tolerate her,—partly for her utility as housekeeper, and partly out of charity. It was only when matters culminated in the Coulombs being expelled, that members began to compare notes, and the exceeding cunning and iniquity of the woman became apparent to all." [1]

This was the woman whom Madame Blavatsky, with characteristic carelessness—sure of her own honesty and ever too trustful of the honesty of others—left in charge of her rooms at Adyar; but she had been sufficiently annoyed by the Harisinghji incident to ask Dr. Hartmann to get rid of the Coulombs before her return.

The threatened revenge was now prepared; while Madame Coulomb was writing to Madame Blavatsky complaints of all at Headquarters, she was speaking to each of these against Madame Blavatsky, and dropping hints as to coming revelations. In sending to Madame Blavatsky an account of all that led up to the dismissal of the Coulombs from Headquarters, Damodar, the most trusted of the Indian workers, wrote on June 14th, 1884, that during this time she implied, though she did not openly state, that "all phenomena were fraud, and that you were an impostor"; she dropped hints about secret passages, trap-doors, etc., she did not use these words, but implied them." "Her sole attempt was to sow seeds of disunion amongst us . . . she attempted to set one member of the Board against another, but ultimately failed ignominiously." The Coulombs would not allow anyone at Headquarters to go into Madame Blavatsky's room—which had always before been freely used by the staff during her frequent absences—and explained the carrying up of workman's tools by the statement that the roof leaked, and that M. Coulomb was mending it. Disgusted with the trouble they were causing, the Board of Control determined to get rid of them; says Dr. Hartmann: "Affidavits sent in by several members went to show that the Coulombs were guilty of gross misconduct, of lying about the Society, slandering its officers, wasting the funds of the Society, etc. We therefore concluded to impeach them in a formal manner." [2] While they were sitting with this object, however, the astral form of a chelâ appeared, and handed to Damodar a note from the Master K.H., addressed to Dr. Hartmann,

---

[1] *Reply to a Report*, etc. Pp. 3-5.

[2] *Report of Observations*, etc. P. 33.

desiring them to carry out reforms, but to be merciful to Madame Coulomb. They obeyed, and dropped the charges, and Dr. Hartmann remarks in a footnote that it was well they did so, as Colonel Olcott's work in Europe would have been seriously interfered with had trouble occurred at Aḍyar at that juncture. [1] For some time after this things went smoothly. A letter of T. V. Charlu's to Madame Blavatsky, dated March 12th, 1884, reports work as going well; Dr. Hartmann had been elected President of the Board of Control, Mr. Lane-Fox was to deliver two lectures in the Patchyappa's Hall, and several of the workers were going up to Ooṭacamunḍ in April, including Madame Coulomb. He mentions the occurrence of two phenomena, two letters received respectively by Prince Harisinghji and Judge Srînivâsa Rao. H. H. the Thakur Saheb of Waḍhwân and Prince Harisinghji had been visiting Headquarters; the latter had put a letter in the Shrine, and later placed on record what occurred. "I was at Headquarters very often during my sojourn with my friend H. H. the Thakur Saheb of Waḍhwân at Maḍras, whither we had gone last March for the celebration of his marriage with the daughter of the Hon. Gajapaṭi Rao. One day I asked Mr. D. M. Mavalankar [Damoḍar] to let me put a letter from me to my revered Master K. H. in the Shrine. It was in a closed envelope, and was regarding private personal matters, which I need not lay before the public. Mr. Damoḍar allowed me to put the letter in the Shrine. The day after, I visited again the Shrine in company with my wife. On opening the Shrine I did find my letter unopened, but addressed to me in blue pencil, while my original superscription, 'My revered Master,' had a pencil line running through it. This was in the presence of Mr. Mavalankar, Dr. Hartmann, and others. The envelope was intact. I opened it, and on the unused portion of my note was an answer from my Master K. H. in His, to me familiar, writing. I should very much like to know how others will explain this, when, as a fact, both the Founders were thousands of miles away. HARISINGHJI RŪPSINGHJI." [2]

A few days after this, Judge Srînivâsa Rao came, and asked to be allowed to sit for awhile before the shrine. Damoḍar took him upstairs and opened the shrine. There was nothing in it beyond its ordinary contents. He was immediately told by his Guru to shut it, and then to re-open. A letter addressed to the Judge lay within.[3]

---

[1] *Ibid.*

[2] *Report of Observations*, etc. P. 57, note.

[3] T. V. Charlu's letter. Judge Srînivâsa Rao's own report has been given previously.

But this calm was deceptive. Colonel Olcott received in London an envelope, post-marked Madras, containing a letter addressed to Madame Coulomb—then at Ootacamund—from Adyar, under date April 28th, 1884, by Dr. Hartmann. It expressed the writer's disbelief in Madame Blavatsky, and alleged that Mr. Lane-Fox had "received secret instructions from the London Fellows" to find out about her trickery. The letter was ill expressed and ill spelt, and the Colonel wrote to Dr. Hartmann, under date July 20th, 1884, that "I offset my personal knowledge of you against this blackguard note." He further said that he had put it away in his dispatch-box, but had noticed that morning on turning over the papers, that the Master had written on it, and that He then told him to send it on to Dr. Hartmann. Dr. Hartmann remarks that the letter was in "a tolerably good imitation of my handwriting." Master M. had written on it: "A clumsy forgery, but good enough to show how much an enterprising enemy can do in that direction. They may call this at Adyar, a pioneer." [1] Truly was it a pioneer of the crop of forged letters published in the Christian College Magazine a few months later, and done by the same hand.

Meanwhile warnings were being given at Adyar. "At about the time when the forged letter was written, I received a letter from a friend in Europe, and when I opened it I found written on the inside in the handwriting of the Master: 'The matter is serious. I will send you a letter through Damodar. Study it carefully,' etc. A few days after this a letter addressed to me dropped into Damodar's room at Ootacamund [Dr. Hartmann was at Adyar,] of which he took notice and then sent it to me, after showing it to Mr. Lane-Fox. It was again in the unmistakable handwriting of the Master. I submit the following extract: 'April 26th, 1884. For some time already the woman has opened communication—a regular diplomatic *pourparler*—with the enemies of the cause, certain padris. She hopes for more than 2000 Rupees from them, if she helps them, ruining, or at least injuring, the Society by injuring the reputation of the Founders. Hence hints as to "trap-doors" and tricks. Moreover when *needed*, trap-doors *will be found*, as they have been forthcoming for some time. They are sole masters of the top storey. They have full entrance to and control of the premises. "Monsieur" is clever and cunning at every handicraft, good mechanic and carpenter and good at walls likewise. *Take note of this, ye Theosophists*. They hate you

---

[1] *The Latest Attack on the Theosophical Society*. Issued by the Council of the London Lodge. Pp. 17, 18.

with the hatred of failure against success; the Society, Henry, H. P. B., Theosophists, and, aye, the very name Theosophy. The—— are ready to lay out a good sum for the ruin of the Society they hate. . . . Moreover the J—— in India are in direct understanding with those of London and Paris. . . . Keep all said above in strictest confidence, if you would be strongest. Let her not suspect you know it, but if you would have my advice be prudent. Yet act without delay. M.'" [1]

Madame Coulomb was at Ooṭacamunḍ. M. Coulomb was at Aḍyar, nibbling at an offer made to him by Dr. Hartmann to go to America; then came a letter from Colonel Olcott, dated Paris, April 2nd, 1884, in which he reproved Madame Coulomb for speaking against the Society and plotting mischief. Back from Ooṭacamunḍ came Madame Coulcomb, Damoḍar and Mr. Lane-Fox; a request from Dr. Hartmann to the Coulombs—still hoping to get rid of them quietly—that they should leave Aḍyar was met with a flat refusal; Madame Blavatsky wrote that she would not return to Aḍyar unless the Coulombs were sent away, and the General Council was called to meet on the 14th May, 1884. The meeting was held and affidavits were presented to it charging: that Madame Coulomb had stated that the object of the Society was to overthrow British Rule in India; that its objects were inimical to true religion; that the phenomena were frauds, and works of the devil; that she had attempted to extort money from members; that she had wasted the Society's funds; that she had been guilty of lying and backbiting; that she had grossly slandered H. P. B.; that her presence at Headquarters was mischievous to the Society. Letters showed that she had sent a black-mailing letter to H. P. B. M. Coulomb was charged with aiding and abetting his wife, and disobeying the orders of the Board of Control. Only the first three charges were tried, and Madame Coulomb neither admitted nor denied them; the evidence was overwhelming, and she was expelled. M. Coulomb was asked to resign, and failing that was expelled, and both were requested to leave. After some further trouble M. Coulomb surrendered the keys of the upper rooms, and Dr. Hartmann, Mr. T. Subba Rao, Judge Srînivâsa Rao, Mr. Brown, Mr. Damoḍar K. Mavalankar and some others, entered the rooms of Madame Blavatsky, from which the Coulombs had excluded all save themselves. Then was seen the work on which M. Coulomb had been engaged. General and Mrs. Morgan had seen the wall intact, and Mrs. Morgan had superintended its papering

[1] *Report of Observations*, etc. Pp. 35, 36.

in December, 1883, as already said. Now, on the side on Madame Blavatsky's bed-room a hole had been broken where the door had once been, and gaped there with broken plaster and rough ends of laths; the wall, as before said, had been lightly built of two partitions of lath and plaster—as there was no support below—separated by a space of twelve inches, partly filled with projecting pieces of laths; the partition on the side of the Occult Room was still intact, but it was evident that the aperture was to have been repeated in the second partition, and presumably the back of the Shrine was to have been made removable, so as to take out and put in objects. In consequence of the Master's warning, however, Dr. Hartmann had "acted without delay," and had stopped the nefarious work before it was completed. The hole in the partition in Madame Blavatsky's bed-room measured 14 inches wide and 27 high, "sufficiently large," says Dr. Hartmann caustically, "for a little boy (who was not afraid of suffocation) to crawl in." A heavy wardrobe covered this hole, and a sliding panel had been made in the back of this wardrobe; the panel was new and very hard to move, yielding with considerable noise to the blows of a mallet. Three other panels, all equally new and stiff, were made in other parts of the two rooms, the purpose of which was not—and is not—clear. "M. Coulomb confessed to having made all these tricks, holes and trap-doors with his own hand, but excused himself by saying that they were made by H. P. Blavatsky's order. He denied having any secret understanding with Missionaries for the purpose of injuring the Society. He then turned over the keys to Mr. Damodar K. Mavalankar, who took possession of the rooms, and it was decided to leave all the holes and sliding panels unrepaired until further decision. It is evident that with very little labor those traps could have been finished and be made to look very suspicious, and we have reason to believe that it was M. Coulomb's intention to finish them before Madame Blavatsky's return from Europe."[1]

In the before-quoted letter of Damodar to Mme. Blavatsky (June 14th, 1884), he relates these occurrences, and says: "We have purposely left the hole and the sliding panels untouched. They bear on their very face the mark of your innocence. The passage behind the Shrine is so small that it is enough to kill a man of suffocation if he were to be two minutes inside. Moreover, it does not communicate with the Shrine. The sliding panels are so new that they can be worked but with force and difficulty, and moreover make a

[1] *Report of Observations*, etc. Pp. 35, 36.

terrible noise. This proves that they could never have been used before."

The Coulombs left Adyar on May 25th, 1884, the first part of the plot having failed by its too prompt discovery. It was, however, to be revived in the future by the agent of the Psychical Research Society, and, owing to his misrepresentation of the facts, few people know that, admittedly at the time, none of these arrangements existed while Mme. Blavatsky was at Adyar, and while the phenomena were occurring, and that all traces of them had been removed before she returned. They were new in May, 1884, and still incomplete, *the wooden back of the Shrine and the wall on which it hung being still intact, so that there was no communication between Mme. Blavatsky's room and the Occult Room.* All was shown to the numerous visitors at Headquarters during the summer of 1884, the wall and panels being left for a time as they were found. Mr. Judge, who came to Adyar on May 26th, thus describes the hole: "It was a rough, unfinished hole in the wall, opening into the space left when the old door had been bricked up. . . . This hole began at the floor, and extended up about 22 inches. From each edge projected pieces of lath, some three inches, others five inches long, so that the opening was thus further curtailed . . . the plaster was newly broken off, the ends of the laths presented the appearance of freshly broken wood, and the wall-paper had been freshly torn off." These facts were seen and signed to by over thirty gentlemen sent for by Mr. Judge as witnesses. Mr. Judge further tells us that, at his request, Mr. Damodar tried to get into the recess through the hole, but could not; Mr. Judge himself tried and failed, as did a "thin coolie;" finally, "a small boy about ten years of age" squeezed in, but found that he could not stand upright, for there were large pieces of hard mortar projecting from the sides. Mr. Judge then sent for a man, who "in my presence bricked up the aperture, re-plastered it, and then re-papered the whole space." And this was done, be it remembered, in the autumn of 1884, before the return of Mme. Blavatsky.

In vain did Madame Coulomb try to make mischief outside. She went to accuse the Society to the Collector of the district—her charge that the T.S. was against British rule was really dangerous—but he told Mr. Lane-Fox that the woman talked such incoherent nonsense that he did not believe a word she said: she was crazy, and he refused to see her when she called again. A Small Cause Judge remarked that the woman must be a lunatic to believe that anyone could be deceived by her tricks. The Missionaries failed to make any capital out of it. "Not one respectable gentleman believes her," writes

Damodar, "but they on the contrary sympathise the more with you and the Society." So hopelessly failed had the attempt, that Madame Coulomb herself disavowed it, and wrote to Madame Blavatsky: "I may have said something in my rage, but I swear on all that is sacred for me that I never said fraud, secret passages, traps, nor that my husband had helped you in any way. If my mouth has uttered these words, I pray to the Almighty to shower on my head the worst maledictions in nature." Foiled for the moment, the Coulombs were not disheartened, and their second attempt was fated to be more successful than the first. M. Coulomb's writing was curiously like that of Madame Blavatsky, Major-General Morgan tells us,[1] and the forged letter sent to London, significantly termed by the Master "a pioneer," indicated the line of the coming attack. In London, the Psychical Research Society, to some extent, apparently, impressed by what they had heard and seen in connexion with Madame Blavatsky—Mr. F. W. Myers having himself seen some phenomena which, he enthusiastically declared, he could never doubt—appointed a Committee to take "such evidence as to the alleged phenomena connected with the Theosophical Society as might be offered by members of that body at the time in England, or as could be collected elsewhere," and this Committee afterwards sent one of their number, Mr. Hodgson, to India to investigate matters on the spot. Meanwhile the Coulombs had been busy; casting about for some way of improving their financial position, and furious with the Society, they approached the Missionaries—Madame Coulomb in the character of a repentant Christian—who had been carrying on a vigorous but unsuccessful crusade against Theosophy. Some twenty letters were offered to the Missionaries, which purported to be written by Madame Blavatsky to Madame Coulomb, in which the former lady unblushingly confessed to a number of frauds, writing to Madame Coulomb as to her confederate. There is some dispute as to the payment made for these; soon after the publication, Prof. Patterson, of the Christian College, Madras, said in answer to a question of Dr. Hartmann, that they had agreed to pay Madame Coulomb Rs. 1000, but had only so far given her Rs. 75; this statement was made in the presence of Mr. Judge, who published it in the *Madras Mail* the following day; General Morgan says that they paid Rs. 150—the sum is unimportant. What is certain is that they bought the letters, and published them in the *Christian College Magazine* for September 1884, and

[1] *Reply to a Report*, etc. P. xvi.

the following months. On the face of them, to anyone acquainted with Madame Blavatsky, the letters are forgeries, for they are the letters of an uneducated woman, whereas the style of Madame Blavatsky was brilliant, however familiar and conversational; they showed ignorance of Indian titles, creating by an absurd blunder, a Mahârâja of Lahore; and they were at once recognised as worthless by those best qualified to judge. Mr. Lane-Fox, writing to the *Times*, stated: "As to the letters purporting to have been written by Madame Blavatsky, which have recently been published in an Indian 'Christian' paper, I, in common with all who are acquainted with the circumstances of the case, have no doubt whatever that, whoever wrote them, they are not written by Madame Blavatsky."

Mr. A. O. Hume, well acquainted with Madame Blavatsky, and not very friendly to her, wrote the following to the Calcutta *Statesman*:

Sir,—I have seen an article in the *Times of India*, referring to certain letters alleged to have been written by Madame Blavatsky to Madame Coulomb, and your brief notice of the same. I desire to warn your readers and the public generally against accepting these supposed letters as altogether genuine. I can do this with the better grace that *all connection between myself, Madame Blavatsky, Col. Olcott, Mr. Damodar, has long since ceased*. I was unable to approve of many things in the conduct of the Society and of its journal, and hence, though still warmly sympathizing in its avowed objects, I have, for the last two years or more, been only a nominal member of the Theosophical Society. It is wholly without bias therefore that I advise all persons interested in the question to suspend their judgments as to the authenticity of these supposed letters. I will not now raise the question as to whether Madame Blavatsky is capable of participating in foolish frauds, such as these letters would make her appear to have directed. All I desire to point out is this: *Madame Blavatsky is no fool;* on the contrary, as all who know her, be they friends or foes, will admit, she is an exceptionally clever and far-sighted woman, with a remarkably keen perception of character. Would such a woman ever give a person like Madame Coulomb the entire power over her future, that the *writing* of such letters involves? Or again, say she *had*, in some mad mood, written such letters, would she have come to an open rupture with the holder of them? Parts of the letters may be genuine enough; one passage cited has a meaning quite different from that in which I see that the *Times of India* accepts it, but believe me, Madame Blavatsky is far too shrewd a woman to have ever *written* to any one, anything that could *convict* her of *fraud*.

ALLAN HUME.

"Simla, September, 1884."

Mr. J. C. Mitter points out the weakness of the allegations: "You will allow that the 'completeness' of the so-called exposure of Madame Blavatsky depends only upon the uncorroborated evidence of one who, according to her own statement, was an active accomplice in the frauds, and who has been aggrieved by expulsion from the Society. A sifting inquiry should be made, and the evidence on both sides heard before judgment is passed, instead of passing our opinion on the statement of an accomplice of whose veracity very little is known, excepting that she herself was a participator in the fraud! Why did not Madame Coulomb publish the letters, &c., she now publishes, immediately she had been ousted from the pale of the Theosophical Society? Was she in need of time for preparation?"

Madame Blavatsky herself met the foul accusation with characteristic indignation and warmth of language: "I swear by the Master whom I serve faithfully, and for the sake of carrying whose orders I suffer now, let Him curse me in the future birth, aye, in a dozen of births, if I have ever done anything on my own hook, if I have ever written one line of these infernal letters. I care not for the experts; I care not for the missionaries, court, jury, or the devil on earth himself. What I tell you now I will maintain in any court before all the Judges of Asia, Europe and America. *I have not written the 'Coulomb letters.'* And if the only person I believe implicitly on earth—MASTER—came and told me I had, then I would lay it at His door; for nothing and no one in this world could have taken away the recollection of that deed—that idiotic, insane deed—from my brain and memory but Himself. So you had better shut up and ask *Him*. The idea of it! Had I been such an ass, I would have never gone to Europe; I would have turned heaven and earth to prevent the Board of Control from turning them out; I would have returned home at the first intimation of danger. . . . I suffer for my misdeeds of centuries ago. I know for *what* I suffer, and bow low my diminished head in humility and resignation. But I bow only to Karma and my Master. I will never bow before the padris or the fear of them. You may publish this letter now, or when I am dead, to let them know." Again: "If you or any one of you verily believe that I was ever guilty consciously of any trick, or that I used the Coulombs as confederates, or any one else, and that I am not quite the victim of the most damnable conspiracy ever set on foot, a conspiracy which was being *prepared for five years*—then telegraph me where I am, *Never show your face again in the Society*, and I will not. Let me perish, but let the Society live and thrive."

It is but a small matter, and yet significant: Would Madame Coulomb, as a confederate in fraud, have written to Madame Blavatsky, on August 13th, 1883: "I verily believe that I shall go silly if I stay with you," relate the Morgan incident, and conclude with, "I say you have dealings with Old Nick," if, at that time, she was a party to fraud, and had herself arranged the phenomenon, as she afterwards pretended? If she were a confederate, she might well have kept up the farce before witnesses, but she certainly would not have kept it up between themselves in private letters, especially at the very time when, according to her, Madame Blavatsky was writing to her with such shameless openness. Such a gratuitous and objectless falsehood as the letter of Aug. 13th is not credible. The letter is quite natural, from a frightened and superstitious Christian; it is incomprehensible from a confederate in an impudent fraud.

No one has ever accused Madame Blavatsky of being a fool, yet only a fool could have penned such insanely compromising letters, and then have quarrelled with the woman who held them. The commonest caution would have prevented such behavior. In 1889, I summed up the evidence on this matter in a letter to the *Methodist Times* (November 28th), and that summary may be reproduced here :—

"Dear Sir,—My attention has been called to a letter from Professor Patterson in your issue of October 31st. My note—to which it is a reply—was called forth by your direct challenge to myself to investigate the evidence against my friend, Madame Blavatsky, and I had no intention of provoking a prolonged correspondence. It is clear that we are face to face with absolutely contradictory assertions. Professor Patterson says Madame Coulomb was not paid for the letters: Major-General Morgan says (pamphlet published in 1884, *Reply to a Report*, etc.) that the Scottish missionaries 'paid them (the Coulombs) Rs. 150 as a commencement.' Professor Patterson says every Theosophist who has expressed a wish to see the letters has been permitted to do so. Madame Blavatsky tells me she asked, and was refused; Mr. B. Keightley tells me he asked, and was refused, and that to his personal knowledge other prominent Theosophists met with the same refusal. I do not know Professor Patterson; I do know these Theosophists; and I prefer to accept their word.

But my belief in the forgery of the letters does not rest on hese comparative trifles; it rests on a review of the whole case. On one side, a man and woman who had been expelled from a Society, the latter for attempts to extort money—four affidavits of such attempts are in evidence; a woman who had been prevented by Madame Blavatsky from obtaining money, and had vowed to be revenged—affidavit giving this threat; a woman who had attempted to blackmail Madame Blavatsky—letter sent by her; a woman who had forged letters from Dr. Hartmann and Major-General Morgan, and who, bringing a suit against the latter for accusing her of forgery, dropped it before it came to trial (the pretence that it was dropped because Madame Blavatsky had left is absurd; what had that lady to do with the forgery of Major-General Morgan's letter?);—a woman who, by her own confession, had been guilty of fraud. On the other side, the evidence of a committee, including Dr. Hartmann, Major-General Morgan, A. J. Cooper-Oakley, Dr. Gebhard, and ten Indian gentlemen of rank, learning and proved ability, who investigated every charge at the time, and declared each one to be fully disproved; the testimony of those who saw the letters that they were manifest forgeries (see Report, 1885); the testimony of Mr. G. Row, 'from my experience as a judicial officer of twenty-five years' standing,' 'I came to the conclusion that every one of the letters was a forgery' (Official Report, 1884); the parallel forgeries on Dr. Hartmann and Major-General Morgan, alleging their disbelief in Madame Blavatsky—forgeries at once denounced and exposed by them on the spot; the internal evidence of the letters, such as the illiterate French, whereas Madame Blavatsky speaks and writes French perfectly, like most educated Russians; the fact that Madame Coulomb was disgraced and expelled, and had everything to gain by currying favour with the missionaries; the fact that the letters were published while Madame Blavatsky was in Europe, that she hurried back to meet the accusation, remained while the matter was investigated, and only left again when the accusations were disproved. (So far from flying secretly, she was assisted into the steamer by the Presidency Magistrate himself, and left at the peremptory order of Dr. Scharlieb, her medical attendant, who feared for her life if she remained in the Madras climate. She had not been called as a witness in the Coulomb-Morgan case, having no concern in it.) I might add to all this the oath of Madame Coulomb: 'I may have said something in my rage, but I swear on all that is sacred for me that I never said fraud, secret passages, traps, nor that my husband had helped you in any way. If my mouth has uttered these words, I pray to the Almighty to shower on my head the worst maledictions in nature.' Emphatic, very; but I do not lay stress on an oath from such lips.

As to Professor Patterson's final threat, let him publish. If any compromising documents existed, those who used Madame Coulomb can have no scruples which would prevent the publication. Madame Blavatsky is poor, a worn-out invalid; she is not likely to go to India to prosecute him.

19, Avenue-road, N.W. ANNIE BESANT."

Madame Blavatsky was eager to prosecute the *Christian College Magazine* for libel, but Colonel Olcott insisted that the matter was one for the Society to decide: "I have represented to Mme. Blavatsky that it is her duty to be governed by the sense of the General Council, and not to undertake to decide for herself. I have told her that she and I, having called into existence this important Society, are now bound to consider ourselves its agents in all things affecting its interests; and that we must subordinate, to the prime question of its welfare, our private reputations, no less than our strength and our means."[1] A committee was appointed, and unanimously decided that she should not prosecute; she reluctantly submitted, only half comforted by the vehement affection and trust shown towards her.

Mr. Hodgson, the gentleman sent by the S.P.R., was present at this memorable Convention Meeting of December, 1884, the Colonel, in the innocence of his heart, extending to him a warm welcome. Mr. Hodgson's appearance of friendship was, however, a mere pretence to cover his real aim; he simulated honest enquiry only the more surely to destroy. A man entrusted with such a task as that confided to Mr. Hodgson should have, above all things, ability, honesty and accuracy. Unfortunately, for himself and all concerned, these special qualities were not prominent in Mr. Hodgson. He was a young man, very sure of himself, and profoundly ignorant of Indian ways and of occult facts; later in life he became convinced of the reality of many forces which he then light-heartedly ridiculed, and of occurrences which he then regarded as impossible, and therefore ignorantly stigmatised as fraud. His evil karma had made him the agent for inflicting a great sorrow on a—in this life—innocent woman, and of striking through her a necessary blow on a great spiritual movement. "The Son of Man indeed goeth as it was written of Him, but woe unto that man by whom the Son of Man is betrayed." Mr. Hodgson had not, before leaving

[1] *Ninth Report of the T.S.*, p. 12. This issue also contains the Report of the Committee.

England, shown any specially brilliant powers, and he came to investigate super-physical occurrences among a people who regarded the English as unworthy to share in their own knowledge, and many of whom, like Mr. T. Subbar Rao, bitterly resented the way in which Madame Blavatsky had thrown aside the veil with which they had covered their secrets from generation to generation. It is indubitable that he, with his English ignorance of Hindu thought and his English contempt for Hindu veracity, was pitted against the brains of the subtlest race in the world, a race, moreover, that to guard its holy things from the insolent foreigner will deny point-blank a belief that will be frankly acknowledged among sympathisers. I do not blame poor Mr. Hodgson that he was befooled to the top of his bent—it may have been more his misfortune than his fault—but I blame him for the prejudice which made him welcome every unproved suspicion or charge made by known enemies of the Theosophical Society, and ignore all evidence tendered by friends. His attitude throughout was not the attitude of the investigator, but that of the sceptic, searching only for proofs of fraud. Mr. Sinnett put the position well, after the issue of Mr. Hodgson's Report. He writes: "Nothing in his Report, even as it now stands—amended with the protracted assistance of more experienced persons unfriendly to the Theosophical movement—suggests that even yet he has begun to understand the primary conditions of the mysteries he set himself to unravel. He has naïvely supposed that every one in India visibly devoted to the work of the Theosophical Society might be assumed, on that account, desirous of securing his good opinion and of persuading him that the alleged phenomena were genuine. He shows himself to have been watching their demeanor and stray phrases to catch admissions that might be turned against the Theosophical case. He seems never to have suspected what any more experienced inquirer would have been aware of from the beginning, that the Theosophical movement, in so far as it has been concerned with making known to the world at large the existence in India of persons called Mahâṭmâs—very far advanced in the comprehension of occult science—and of the philosophical views they hold, has been one which many of the native devotees of these Mahâṭmâs and many among the most ardent disciples and students of their occult teaching, have regarded with profound irritation. The traditional attitude of mind in which Indian occultists regard their treasures of knowledge, is one in which devotion is largely tinged with jealousy of all who would endeavor to penetrate the secrecy in which these treasures have hitherto been shrouded. These have been regarded as only the rightful acquirement of persons passing through the usual ordeals and probations. The Theosophical movement in India, however, involved a breach of this secrecy. The old rules were infringed under an authority so great that occultists who found themselves entangled with the work could not but submit. But in many cases such submission has been no more than superficial. Any one more intimately acquainted than the agent of the S.P.R. with the history and growth of the Theosophical Society would have been able to indicate many persons among its most faithful native members, whose fidelity was owing entirely to the Masters they served, and not to the idea on which they were employed—at all events not so far as it was connected with the demonstration of the fact that abnormal physical phenomena could be produced by Indian proficients in occult science. Now for such persons the notion that European outsiders, who had, as they conceived, so undeservedly been admitted to the inner arcana of Eastern occultism, were blundering into the belief that they had been deceived—that there was no such thing as Indian occultism, that the Theosophical movement was a sham and a delusion with which they would no more concern themselves—was enchanting in its attractions; and the arrival in their midst of an exceedingly self-reliant young man from England attempting the investigation of occult mysteries by the methods of a Scotland Yard detective, and laid open by total unfamiliarity with the tone and temper of modern occultism to every sort of misapprehension, was naturally to them a source of intense satisfaction. Does the committee of the S.P.R. imagine that the native occultists of the Theosophical Society in India are writhing at this moment under the judgment it has passed? I am quite certain, on the contrary, that for the most part they are chuckling over it with delight. They may find the situation complicated as regards their relations with their Masters in so far as they have consciously contributed to the easy misdirection of Mr. Hodgson's mind, but the ludicrous spectacle of himself which Mr. Hodgson furnishes in his Report—where we see him catching up unfinished sentences and pointing out weak places in the evidence of some among the Indian chelâs, against whom, if he had better understood the task before him, he ought to have been most on his guard—is, at all events, one which we can understand them to find amusing." [1]

After the competency of the reporter, his honesty is the

[1] *The Occult World Phenomena.* By A. P. Sinnett. Pp. 2-4.

next point of importance. Was Mr. Hodgson honest? On this, I regret to say, there is one convincing proof in the negative, a fact that I published in March, 1891, in a then well-known Magazine, *Time*, and which, so far as I know, has never been contradicted; it is, in fact, incapable of contradiction. Mr. Hodgson, in his Report, publishes a "plan of the Occult Room with shrine and surroundings (from measurements taken by R. Hodgson, assisted by the statements of Theosophic witnesses)." On p. 220 Mr. Hodgson says that "the accompanying rough sketch, made from measurements of my own, shows the positions." The reader will now see why I laid stress on the fact that Mr. Judge had, in the summer of 1884, bricked up the hole, plastered the wall, and then re-papered it; this having been done in the summer of 1884, how could Mr. Hodgson have made a rough sketch of the positions from his own measurements in the spring of 1885? It may be asked: "How then did Mr. Hodgson obtain his plan?" The answer is simple; Mr. Judge gives it. He says: "I made a plan of how it had been left by Coulomb, and that plan it is that Hodgson pirated in his report, and desires people to think his, and to be that which he made on the spot, while looking at that which he thus pretends to have drawn." All that Mr. Hodgson could have seen was a blank wall. I reprint here the comment I made in *Time* on this remarkable proceeding: "I venture to suggest that the pirating of another person's plan, with 'measurements' of things that no longer existed when Mr. Hodgson visited Adyar, is not consistent with good faith. Yet the whole terrible charge against Mme. Blavatsky rests on this man's testimony. The Society of Psychical Research, which has taken the responsibility of the report, has no knowledge of the facts, other than that afforded by Mr. Hodgson. Everything turns on his veracity. And he issues another man's plan as his own, and makes imaginary measurements of vanished objects."

Thirdly, was Mr. Hodgson accurate, or was he hasty and slipshod? A single instance will suffice to show the extreme carelessness with which he flung out accusations. Mr. Mohini M. Chatterji makes the following remarks on pp. 357-8 of the Report: "Briefly stated, the phenomenon consisted in my hearing at the same time two voices—Madame Blavatsky's and another—while sitting with her alone in her room in the house of the late Mr. Nobin K. Bannerji *at Darjiling*. 'Concerning this incident,' Mr. Hodgson says, 'I need only remind the reader of the hollow in the wall which was near the corner of Madame Blavatsky's room. The confederate may have been Babula, previously instructed in the reply, and with a mangoe-leaf in his mouth to disguise his voice.' In regard to this hypothesis I, in my turn, need only remind the reader that the incident did not take place at Maḍras, where Mr. Hodgson examined Madame Blavatsky's rooms, but *at Darjiling*, in the Himâlayas, months before the house at Maḍras was bought or occupied. What light is thrown on Mr. Hodgson's conclusions by this inaccuracy, after all his patient and searching enquiry, in which great attention is always professed to have been paid to facts, I leave others to determine." [1]

The first point made in the Report is the presence of trap-doors, and other arrangements for fraud in the rooms occupied by Madame Blavatsky at Aḍyar. This presence is fully explained in the preceding pages, which make it abundantly clear that if—contrary to all the evidence—Madame Blavatsky had contemplated the use of these fraudulent means for performing phenomena, that use lay in the future, as these appliances were not in existence when she left India, February, 1884, and were not completed and ready for use even in May, 1884, when they were discovered. But if this be true—and the truth of it is abundantly proven—what becomes of Mr. Hodgson's detailed account of the elaborate arrangement by which a communication was made between Madame Blavatsky's bed-room and the inside of the cupboard—the Shrine—in the Occult Room? He alleges that the top half of the panel at the back of the cupboard was made to slide—Mr. Hodgson did not see the cupboard, and Dr. Hartmann, who did see it and examine it, says it had "a solid, unmovable back," [2] and this is confirmed by others; a mirror was hung in the cupboard to hide the line of separation—no one has ever mentioned this mirror, but there was one on a wall at right-angles, concealing another sliding panel, which was, however, visible in the hall outside; a hole was made through the wall—this was never made, as we have seen; next a panel in the

[1] *The Occult World Phenomena.* P. 47.

[2] "The so-called 'shrine' was a simple cupboard hung loosely to a wall in Madame Blavatsky's room. I examined it on this occasion [the evening of his arrival] and more carefully afterwards, and found it like any other cupboard provided with shelves, and a solid unmovable back, hung upon an apparently solid and plastered wall. However, as a door had been in that wall before, which, as Madame Blavatsky told me, had been walled up, and as a wall without any adequate support from below would be so very heavy that the joists upon which it rested might give way, the interior of the wall was not filled up with bricks, but was left hollow, leaving a space between the bricks of some twelve inches in depth." (*Report of Observations*, etc. P. 12).

blocked-up door was made to slide—this is presumably the hole made in the partition, the door having been removed; lastly a sliding panel was made in the back of the wardrobe. If anyone went into the wardrobe, opened the back of the wardrobe and the panel of the door—with blows of a mallet, to announce his coming?—he could slip into the space between the door and the brickwork—if a very small boy, who did not object to suffocation—and then, through the hole in the brickwork, slide up the top of the panel in the cupboard—which would thus appear to the expectant letter-receiver in the Occult Room, and explain the blows of the mallet—and come on the back of the mirror—on the other wall of the room; and push it aside. All this Mr. Hodgson learned from the veracious M. Coulomb, and *from nobody else*. If M. Coulomb had added that this was his plan, although he had unfortunately been interrupted in its execution, all would have been sufficiently probable; Madame Coulomb had been a medium in Cairo, of not very good reputation, and M. Coulomb may have acquired his carpentering skill and his ingenious ideas in her service; the Coulombs may even have thought of utilising the Shrine—with its already high reputation—for phenomena of their own, with the view of increasing their slender resources; for Madame Blavatsky tells how angry Madame Coulomb often was with her, because she would never show any phenomena for money, nor produce them in a way to bring about gifts. Madame Coulomb could not see the sense of neglecting such an obvious way of filling an often depleted exchequer, and it is possible that the making of holes and sliding panels was intended for the use of the Coulombs only, with a view to extracting cash from the pockets of recalcitrant Indian Princes, rather than as an elaborate plot against Mme. Blavatsky. On the whole of this matter, Mr. Hodgson simply repeats M. Coulomb; he is not a judge, but a mouth-piece of an accuser—a *soi-disant* accomplice, turned King's evidence. "M. Coulomb states," a "statement of M. Coulomb," "according to M. Coulomb"—such are the reiterated assertions. And of evidence of these frauds outside this tainted source—none.

It may be worth while to complete the evidence destroying this part of Mr. Hodgson's case—or that of the Coulombs, as they are identical—by a statement made by Mr. Gribble, "the gentleman employed by the missionaries as an expert" in connection with the forged letters. After their publication, he visited Adyar to inspect the "machinery for trickery" which, it was stated, in the *Christian College Magazine*, "undoubtedly exists, and is admirably adapted for the production of the

Adyar phenomena. Two theories are possible respecting it. Either: (1) It was constructed for, and used by Madame Blavatsky in the production of these phenomena; or, (2) It was constructed after Madame Blavatsky's departure, in order to ruin her reputation." There is a third possibility, the one just suggested, that it may have been meant for the private use of the Coulombs during Madame Blavatsky's frequent absences. The first theory has been proved to be false, as the wall and back of the Shrine were both intact after, as well as before, she left Adyar. The second theory, therefore, holds the ground. Mr. Gribble says: "I was also shown two of the sliding doors and panels said to have been made by M. Coulomb after Madame Blavatsky's departure. One of these is on the outside of the so-called Occult Room upstairs. Both of these have been made without the slightest attempt at concealment. The former is at the top of a back staircase, and consists of two doors which open into a kind of bookshelf."

There was a book-case on the wall separating the Occult Room from the outer hall, and this panel was behind a mirror, hanging between the two parts of the book-case, with a shelf in front of it; this is probably the mirror spoken of by M. Coulomb to Mr. Hodgson, removed into the Shrine, for the sake of the story. To proceed with Mr. Gribble: "This gives the idea of having been constructed so as to place food on the shelves inside, without opening the door.[1] The other contrivance is a sliding panel which lifts up,[2] and opens and shuts with some difficulty. It is evidently of recent construction. Certainly in its present state it would be difficult to carry out any phenomena by its means. Neither of these two appliances communicates with the shrine, which is situated on the cross-wall dividing the Occult Room from an adjoining bedroom." [3] Mr. Gribble appears to have been a veritable Balaam, brought by the missionaries to curse their enemies, and blessing them instead.

Surely, with this overwhelming evidence, from so many sources, opposed to the one statement of M. Coulomb, written down by Mr. Hodgson, we ought to hear no more about fraudulent phenomena connected with the Shrine in the Occult Room at Adyar.

A final paragraph may be added on this part of the case:

---

[1] This idea of the good missionary-agent will doubtless recommend itself to Hindus, who are accustomed to having food handed into their pûjâ rooms!

[2] Probably the one intended for the back of the Shrine.

[3] *Report of the Result*, etc. P. 103.

the Shrine was not fastened to the wall, as we have seen, but was merely hanging thereon and was easily removable. Would anyone out of Bedlam have concocted an elaborate apparatus for the fraudulent production of phenomena within it, and then have allowed it to hang loosely over the opening, so that anyone could peep behind it and see the opening, or might remove it and expose the whole affair? Apart from this, Madame Blavatsky was surrounded with phenomena wherever she went, and the Shrine was only made in 1883, after she went to Adyar; she could only at most have used it for the few months during which she was staying there, and its presence cannot explain the phenomena which are borne witness to by reputable American, European and Indian gentlemen, from 1874 to 1882. Moreover, the phenomena in connection with the Shrine also occurred after she had left Adyar for Europe. It is necessary, if the S.P.R. Report is to be credited, not only to condemn Madame Blavatsky as a fraud, but to condemn also the honorable gentlemen associated with her during all these years, as her fellow-conspirators and cheats. Even if they were her dupes while she was present, they must have become active participants in fraud when she was absent.

Mr. Hodgson's second charge consists of the forged letters produced by Madame Coulomb, and alleged by her to have come from Madame Blavatsky. The only evidence for their genuineness is the word of Madame Coulomb, and the opinion of two experts, Messrs. Netherclift & Sims. This opinion is much discounted by the fact that Mr. Netherclift and Mr. Sims—in this matter of the recognition of Madame Blavatsky's writing—varied and contradicted themselves; Mr. Hodgson submitted to them some writing which he thought was done by her, and was "surprised to find" that they thought it was not hers. When, however, this *same writing* was "re-submitted to him" (Mr. Netherclift) he thought that it was hers "without doubt," Mr. Sims complaisantly changing his opinion also. The value of such expert opinion was well shown in the suit brought by Mr. Parnell against the *Times*; the *Times* had been duped, as Mr. Hodgson was, by a clever forger, and paid heavily for its trust in experts of the Netherclift type. Their evidence was proved to be worthless, and the forger, convicted of fraud, made the public apology of suicide. Mr. Montague Williams, Q.C., the eminent counsel, relates a case in which this same Mr. Netherclift and another expert swore positively to some writing as that of one man, while it was proved to be that of another; he considers their evidence on handwriting to be worthless, and says: "In my opinion they are utterly unreliable."[1] Yet this utterly unreliable man, with his worthless evidence, is to be held to outweigh the great mass of testimony to the obvious identity of the writing in the letters received through Madame Blavatsky, and those received far away from her. Against Madame Coulomb's word and the worthless opinion of the experts, I place the evidence given above on pp. 17-20, and contentedly leave the public to form its own opinion.

Mr. Hodgson's third charge is that certain letters alleged to be from the Mahâṭmâ Kooṭ Hoomi were written by Madame Blavatsky, or in some cases by Damoḍar. With regard to this young Hinḍu gentleman it may be said that he gave up family, wealth, and friends and became an outcaste, in order to devote himself to ceaseless work and hardships of all kinds, for the sake of the Theosophical Society. He lost everything for it, and only gained—his Master.

The gain, truly, outweighed a million times the loss, *if the gain were real.* But on the hypothesis that Damoḍar made himself a party to a fraud, postulating a non-existent Master, one asks oneself: "To what end?" The high-class Brâhmana does not readily live and eat with Europeans, and become impoverished and an outcaste for their sake. Is it conceivable that he would suffer thus, in order to take part in a fraud which gave him nothing? At any rate, he believed in the fraud sufficiently strongly to leave Aḍyar, when he became convinced that Madame Blavatsky would not return, to travel northwards, to plunge into the fastnesses of the Himâlayas, and to climb over their snow-covered passes, in order to find the hermitage of Him in whom he believed. Thus he passed out of the story of the Society.

The before-mentioned experts varied together as to the authorship of the letters submitted to them; first they said they were not done by Madame Blavatsky; then, this not satisfying Mr. Hodgson, they said they were. As against this variable opinion of theirs may be put that of Herr Ernst Schütze, the Court expert in caligraphy at Berlin, who gave evidence on oath that the letter of Master K. H. "has not the remotest resemblance with the letter of Madame Blavatsky," and who wrote: "I must assure you most positively that if you have believed that both letters came from one and the same hand, you have labored under a most complete mistake." Mr. Hodgson has made a minute examination of the letters and thinks that she wrote them; dozens of other people have come to the exactly opposite

---

[1] *Leaves from a Life* P. 263.

conclusion. Certainly, on the surface, the two handwritings are as different as any two could be, and when we remember the immense mass of such letters received through her, it is difficult to conceive it to be possible that she should have written these innumerable sheets of MS without a falter, in the clear beautiful hand so unlike her own by no means admirable, though characteristic, caligraphy. But the really insuperable difficulty which lies in the way of Mr. Hodgson's theory is that letters in this same beautiful and delicate script came to people in all sorts of ways in which Madame Blavatsky could, by no possibility, have taken part. Such letters were received, not by post, when she was thousands of miles away, and I have given above a number of cases of such writing having been received where it was physically impossible that she could have had anything to do with it. These are the solid facts placed against Mr. Hodgson's suppositions.

The airy and baseless character of his assumptions, in the absence of facts, strikes strangely on the sober reader. "It may have thus"; "it is probable that"; "it may be suggested"; so and so "may have done" such a thing. These are the variations from quotations from M. Coulomb.

The one really original idea in the Report is the motive suggested by Mr. Hodgson for Mme. Blavatsky's alleged proceedings. Here is a Russian lady, of admittedly high birth and social position, playing the fool in Europe, America and India, to her own financial and social ruin, gaining nothing but abuse and slander, when she might be living luxuriously in high dignity in her own land. Mr. Hodgson rejects the idea that she is a religious monomaniac; he admits that pecuniary gain was not her object, and discards the theory of a "morbid yearning for notoriety." "A casual conversation opened" his eyes at last, and he discovered the secret of her strange career: she was a Russian agent, and "her ultimate object has been the furtherance of Russian interests." This sapient conclusion is, perhaps, the best criterion of Mr. Hodgson's ability, the more so as it is partly based on a "fragmentary script which forms one of the Blavatsky-Coulomb documents"—in plain English, a torn scrap picked out of Madame Blavatsky's waste-paper basket by Madame Coulomb.

Mr. Sinnett cruelly strikes down this great discovery in an indignant protest against the S.P.R. for publishing, "with all the authority their proceedings can confer, a groundless and monstrous invention concerning Mme. Blavatsky, which Mr. Hodgson puts forward at the conclusion of his report to prop up its obvious weakness as regards the whole hypothesis on which it rests. For it is evident that there is a powerful presumption against any theory that imputes conscious imposture and vulgar trickery to a person who, on the face of things, has devoted her life to a philanthropic idea, at the manifest sacrifice of all the considerations which generally supply motives of action to mankind. Mr. Hodgson is alive to the necessity of furnishing Mme. Blavatsky with a motive as degraded as the conduct he has been taught by M. and Mme. Coulomb to believe her guilty of, and he triumphs over the difficulty by suggesting that she may be a Russian political agent, working in India to foster disloyalty to the British Government. It is nothing to Mr. Hodgson that she has notoriously been doing the reverse; that she has frequently assured the natives orally, by writings, at public meetings, and in letters that can be produced, that with all its faults the British Government is the best available for India, and repeatedly from the point of view of one speaking *en connaissance de cause* she has declared that the Russian would be immeasurably worse. It is nothing to Mr. Hodgson that her life has been passed *coram populo* to an almost ludicrous extent, ever since she has been in India, that her whole energies and work have been employed on the Theosophic cause, or that the Government of India, after looking into the matter with the help of its police when she first came to the country, soon read the riddle aright, and abandoned all suspicion of her motives. Mr. Hodgson is careless of the fact that everyone who has known her for any length of time laughs at the absurdity of his hypothesis. He has obtained from his guide and counsellor—Mme. Coulomb—a fragment of Mme. Blavatsky's handwriting, picked up, it would seem, some years ago, and cherished for any use that might ultimately be made of it—which refers to Russian politics, and reads like part of an argument in favor of the Russian advance in Central Asia. This is enough for the Psychical Researcher, and the text of this document appears in his Report in support of his scandalous insinuation against Mme. Blavatsky's integrity. The simple explanation of the paper is that it is evidently a discarded fragment from a long translation of Colonel Grodekoff's Travels in Central Asia (or whatever title the series bore) which Mme. Blavatsky made at my request for the *Pioneer* (the Indian Government organ), of which I was at that time Editor. I will not delay this pamphlet to write to India and get the dates at which the Grodekoff series of articles appeared in the *Pioneer*. They ran for some weeks, and must have appeared in one of the latter years of the last decade, or possibly in 1880. By applying to the *Pioneer* printers, Mr. Hodgson could perhaps obtain, if the MS. of this translation has been preserved, several hundred pages of Mme. Blavatsky's writing, blazing with sentiments of the most ardent Anglo-phobia. It is most likely, as I say, that the pilfered slip of which he is so proud, was some rejected page from that translation, unless, indeed, which would be more amusing still, it should happen to have fallen from some other Russian translations which Mme. Blavatsky, to my certain knowledge, once made for the Indian Foreign Office during one of her visits to Simla, when she made the acquaintance of some of the officials in that department, and was employed to do some work in its service.

"I venture to think that if Madame Blavatsky had not been known to be too ill supplied with money to claim redress at the costly bar of British justice—if she had *not* been steeped to the lips in the flavor, so ungrateful to British law courts, of psychic mystery, the committee of the S.P.R. would hardly have thought it well to accuse her, in a published document, of infamous conduct, which, if she were really guilty of it, would render her a public foe in the land of her adoption and an object of scorn to honorable men—at the flippant suggestion of their private agent in desperate need of an explanation for conclusions which no amount of pedantically ordered circumstances could render, without it, otherwise than incredible." [1]

It was, as a matter of fact, part of the translation of Grodekoff's *Travels*, which Mr. Hodgson obtained from Madame Coulomb. This is the only motive that Mr. Hodgson can discover for the frauds of which he accuses her, and these, be it remembered, must have been begun in America in 1874. If the Report should live, through its connexion with the noble woman whom it slanders, surely, in the centuries to come, this charge of Mr. Hodgson's will be met with inextinguishable laughter, and men will wonder at the folly of those who gave any credit to this young man.

Mr. Hodgson's Report was presented to his Committee, consisting of Messrs. E. Gurney, F. W. H. Myers, F. Podmore, H. Sidgwick and J. H. Stack, and these gentlemen, on June 24th, 1885, announced their agreement with its conclusions. The Report itself was published in the December number of the Society's *Proceedings*. Mr. Sinnett comments very strongly, but not too strongly, on the utter unfairness of the Committee's action, and indeed it is hard to understand—were not history full of similar injustices perpetrated on those who are ahead of their time—how such men as are named above could lend themselves to, and lead their Society into, the unjust

[1] *The Occult World Phenomena*. Pp. 9-11.

and cruel action of the publication of this infamous Report. Mr. Sinnett says: "I regard the committee of the S.P.R.—Messrs. E. Gurney, F. W. H. Myers, F. Podmore, H. Sidgwick and J. H. Stack—much more to blame for presuming to pass judgment by the light of their own unaided reflections on the raw and misleading report supplied to them by Mr. Hodgson, than he for his part is to blame, even for misunderstanding so lamentably the problems he set out naturally ill-qualified to investigate. It would have been easy for them to have called in any of several people in London, qualified to do so by long experience of the Theosophical movement, to report in their turn on the *prima facie* case, so made out against the authenticity of the Theosophical phenomena, before proceeding to pass judgment on the whole accusation in the hearing of the public at large. We have all heard of cases in which judges think it unnecessary to call on the defence; but these have generally been cases in which the judges have decided against the theory of the prosecution. The committee of the S.P.R. furnish us with what is probably an unprecedented example of a judicial refusal to hear a defence on the ground that the *ex parte* statement of the prosecutor has been convincing by itself. The committee brooded, however, in secret over the report of their agent, consulted no one in a position to open their eyes as to the erroneous method in which Mr. Hodgson had gone to work, and concluded their but too independent investigation by denouncing as one of the most remarkable impostors of history, a lady held in the highest honour by a considerable body of persons, including old friends and relations of unblemished character, and who has undeniably given up station and comfort to struggle for long years in the service of the Theosophical cause amidst obloquy and privation."

He speaks contemptuously, with reference to the attack upon himself, made in the same Report, of "the whole catalogue of minute conjectures which Mr. Hodgson has put together in his Report, while abusing the hospitality which was extended to him at the Headquarters of the Theosophical Society at Adyar, and while leading the guileless representatives of the movement in Madras to suppose, that by opening their hearts and records to his inspection, by giving him the free-est access to their apartments and their diaries, they would best persuade him of the simple truthfulness of their lives, and the improbability that they were slaving amidst penury and self-sacrifice for the propagation of an empty delusion and the cruel deception of their best friends."[1]

[1] *The Occult World Phenomena*. Pp. 7, 8 and 12.

Needless to say, the issue of the *Proceedings* raised a storm, and for a time it seemed as though the Society would be slain by the blow. Not only the outer world, ever ready to believe evil, welcomed the idea that the superphysical marvels were fraudulent, but many of the members of the Society fell away. Madame Blavatsky writes: "Our Fellows, influenced by Hodgson and Hume, begin, or have already, 'lost confidence in the Founders.' Mistakes were made, showing that we are not protected by the Mahâṭmâs. Indeed? And the chief mistake is pointed out as being that of having taken in and kept for five years the Coulombs. 'How could the Mahâṭmâs allow this, knowing they were such rascals, and foreseeing things, if They do foresee?' is asked. As well accuse the first Christians of believing in Christ and His phenomena when he kept Judas for three years as His Disciple, to be betrayed by, and crucified through, him. 'Feed even the hungry snake, without fear of its bite,' said the Lord Buddha. 'Help the hungry spirits (pisâchas); never refuse hospitality to the homeless, or food to the hungry, for fear that he might thank you by robbing or murdering you.' Such is the policy of the Mahâṭmâs. The karma of the Coulombs is theirs, ours is our own. I would do it over again. There are periods of probation for Societies as well as for individual members. If the latter have misunderstood the Mahâṭmâs and Their policy it is their, not our, fault. The Masters will not interfere with karma."

Of all the accusations made against her the one that most wounded her sense of pride and dignity was Mr. Hodgson's dastard allegation that she was a Russian spy. She declared that unless she were allowed to sue him for libel on this, she would never return to India—and she never did. Mr. Sinnett—who stood gallantly by her through this bitter storm—printed in his pamphlet, *The Occult World Phenomena*, a protest from her pen. I give it here:

MADAME BLAVATSKY'S PROTEST.

"The 'Society for Psychical Research' have now published the Report made to one of their Committees by Mr. Hodgson, the agent sent out to India to investigate the character of certain phenomena, described as having taken place at the Headquarters of the Theosophical Society in India and elsewhere, and with the production of some of which I have been directly or indirectly concerned. This Report imputes to me a conspiracy with the Coulombs and several Hindus to impose on the credulity of various persons around me by fraudulent devices, and declares to be genuine a series of letters alleged to be written by me to Mme. Coulomb in connection with the supposed conspiracy, which letters I have already myself declared to be in large part fabrications. Strange to say, from the time the investigation was begun, fourteen months ago, and to this day, when I am declared guilty by my self-instituted judges, I was never permitted to see those incriminating letters. I draw the attention of every fair-minded and *honorable Englishman* to this fact.

"Without at present going into a minute examination of the errors, inconsistencies, and bad reasoning of this Report, I wish to make as publicly as possible my indignant and emphatic protest against the gross aspersions thus put upon me by the Committee of the Psychical Research Society at the instigation of the single, incompetent, and unfair inquirer whose conclusions they have accepted. There is no charge against me in the whole of the present Report that could stand the test of an impartial inquiry on the spot, where my own explanations could be checked by the examination of witnesses. They have been developed in Mr. Hodgson's own mind, and kept back from my friends and colleagues while he remained at Madras abusing the hospitality and unrestrained assistance in his inquiries supplied to him at the Headquarters of the Society at Adyar, where he took up the attitude of a friend, though he now represents the persons with whom he thus associated—as cheats and liars. These charges are now brought forward supported by the one-sided evidence collected by him, and when the time has gone by at which even he could be confronted with antagonistic evidence and with arguments with which his very limited knowledge of the subject he attempted to deal with do not supply him. Mr. Hodgson, having thus constituted himself prosecutor and advocate in the first instance, and having dispensed with a defence in the complicated transactions he was investigating, finds me guilty of all the offences he has imputed to me in his capacity as judge, and declares that I am proved to be an arch-impostor.

"The Committee of the P. R. S. have not hesitated to accept the general substance of the judgment which Mr. Hodgson thus pronounces, and have insulted me publicly by giving their opinion in favor of their agent's conclusions—an opinion which rests wholly and solely on the Report of their single deputy.

"Wherever the principles of fairness and honorable care for the reputation of slandered persons may be understood, I think the conduct of the Committee will be regarded with some feeling resembling the profound indignation of which I am sensible. That Mr. Hodgson's elaborate but misdirected inquiries, his affected precision, which spends infinite patience over trifles and is blind to facts of importance, his contradictory reasoning and his manifold incapacity to deal with such problems as those he endeavored to solve, will be exposed by other writers in due course, I make no doubt. Many friends who know me better than the Committee of the P. R. S. will remain unaffected by the opinions of that body, and in their hands I must leave my much-abused reputation. But one passage in this monstrous Report I must, at all events, answer in my own name.

"Plainly alive to the comprehensive absurdity of his own conclusions about me as long as they remained totally unsupported by any theory of a motive which could account for my life-long devotion to my Theosophical work at the sacrifice of my natural place in society in my own country, Mr. Hodgson has been base enough to concoct the assumption that I am a Russian political agent, inventing a sham religious movement for the sake of undermining the British Government in India! Availing himself, to give color to this hypothesis, of an old bit of my writing, apparently supplied to him by Madame Coulomb, but which he did not know to be as it was, *a fragment of an old translation* I made for the *Pioneer* from some Russian travels in Central Asia, Mr. Hodgson has promulgated this theory about me in the Report, which the gentlemen of the S. P. R. have not been ashamed to publish. Seeing that I was naturalised nearly eight years ago a citizen of the United States, which led to my losing every right to my pension of 5,000 roubles yearly as the widow of a high official in Russia; that my voice has been invariably raised in India to answer all native friends that bad as I think the English Government in some respects—by reason of its unsympathetic character—the Russian would be a thousand times worse; that I wrote letters to that effect to Indian friends before I left America on my way to India, in 1879; that every one familiar with my pursuits and habits and very undisguised life in India, is aware that I have no taste for or affinity with politics whatever, but an intense dislike to them; that the Government of India, which suspected me as a spy because I was a Russian, when I first went to India, soon abandoned its needless *espionage*, and has never, to my knowledge, had the smallest inclination to suspect me since—the Russian spy theory about me which Mr. Hodgson has thus resuscitated from the grave, where it had been buried with ridicule for years, will merely help to render his extravagant conclusions about me more stupid even than they would have been otherwise in the estimation of my friends, and of all who really know me. But looking upon the character of a spy with the disgust which only a Russian who is *not* one can feel, I am impelled irresistibly to repudiate Mr. Hodgson's groundless and infamous calumny with a concentration of the general contempt his method of procedure in this inquiry seems to me to merit, and to be equally deserved by the Committee of the Society he has served. They have shown themselves, by their wholesale adoption of his blunders, a group of persons less fitted to explore the mysteries of psychic phenomena than I should have thought—in the present day, after all that has been written and published on the subject of late years—could have been found among educated men in England.

"Mr. Hodgson knows, and the Committee doubtless share his knowledge, that he is safe from actions for libel at my hands, because I have no money to conduct costly proceedings (having given all I ever had to the cause I serve), and also because my vindication would involve the examination into psychic mysteries which cannot be dealt fairly with in a court of law; and again because there are questions which I am solemnly pledged never to answer, but which a legal investigation of these slanders would inevitably bring to the front, while my silence and refusal to answer certain queries would be misconstrued into 'contempt of court.' This condition of things explains the shameless attack that has been made upon an almost defenceless woman, and the inaction in face of it to which I am so cruelly condemned.

Jan. 14, 1886. H. P. BLAVATSKY."

There was one policy with regard to the Masters, the phenomena worked by her, and Their communications, which she would not tolerate: the attempts to separate the occult from the philosophical, and to evade the criticism and the hostility of an ignorant world by exalting the philosophical at the expense of the occult. To do this, she repeatedly declared, was to invite the destruction of the Society. She was bitterly conscious of the unfairness with which she had been treated, and of the way in which many Theosophists were willing to sacrifice her to the mob, while profiting by her teachings, and declaring that the Theosophical Society had its own foundation, and could continue to exist, even if she were regarded as a fraud. Protesting against this, she wrote to Adyar from Switzerland, declaring that while she was ready to sacrifice her life and her honor for the sake of the Society, it meant death to the Society if the manifestations of the Masters and Their communications to members were to be given up as fraudulent; she quoted with approval those who "tell me that the T.S., minus Masters, is an absurdity; and that I am their only means of communication with the Masters and for giving out Their philosophy—the Society, unless I work for it as in the past, is a dead thing." That the Society was only worthy to live, if it were a witness to and a channel for the Masters' teachings, was her constant declaration, and she only cared for it as an instrument for carrying out Their work in the world.

What H. P. Blavatsky was the world may some day know. She was of heroic stature, and smaller souls instinctively resented her strength, her titanic nature. Unconventional, careless of appearances, frank to unwisdom—as the world estimates wisdom—too honest to calculate against the dishonesty of others, she laid herself open to continual criticism and misunderstanding. Full of intellectual strength and with extraordinary knowledge, she was humble as a little child. Brave to recklessness, she was pitiful and tender. Passionately indignant when accused of sins she loathed, she was generous and forgiving to a repentant foe. She had a hundred splendid virtues, and a few petty failings. May the Master she served with unfaltering courage, with unwavering devotion, send back to us again "the Brother you know as H. P. B., but we—otherwise."